Childhood Sleep Disorders

Childhood Sleep Disorders

Connie J. Schnoes, PhD

MP MOMENTUM PRESS
HEALTH

First published in 2017 by
Momentum Press®, LLC
222 East 46th Street, New York, NY 10017
www.momentumpress.net

ISBN-13: 978-1-94474-937-8 (print)
ISBN-13: 978-1-94474-938-5 (e-book)

Momentum Press Child Clinical Psychology "Nuts and Bolts" Collection

Cover and interior design by S4Carlisle Publishing Services Private Ltd., Chennai, India

First edition: 2017

10 9 8 7 6 5 4 3 2 1

Printed in the United States of America

Dedication

*I dedicate this book to my husband, Dan, our children,
Whitney, Jordan, Morgan, Paige, Abby and Colin, and my parents,
James and Marilyn. All of you compel me to be the best person
I can be and are God's greatest gifts to me.*

Abstract

Childhood Sleep Disorders is a thorough introduction to pediatric sleep disorders. The book focuses on behavioral pediatric sleep disorders with guidance for sleep disorders that have a medical component. Readers will learn about the key factors contributing to the etiology, assessment and treatment of sleep disorders in children.

Childhood Sleep Disorders addresses the importance of sleep for the emotional, physical and behavioral health and development of children. Trends in sleep habits, barriers to healthy sleep and recommended total sleep time are discussed. Establishing healthy sleep habits and sleep hygiene is discussed.

Case examples are provided to illustrate the application of the information discussed in the conceptualization, assessment and treatment chapters. The case examples provided include young children and teens who present with various sleep disorders as well as with comorbid anxiety. Case conceptualizations are discussed to demonstrate the formulation of comprehensive sleep intervention protocols.

Keywords

adolescents, bedtime resistance, behavioral insomnia of childhood, children, insomnia, night terrors, night wakings, parasomnias, sleep, sleep deprivation

Contents

Acknowledgments

I would like to acknowledge Pat Friman and Brett Kuhn. Pat and Brett, you have been tremendous mentors in my life and were instrumental in my introduction to the psychology of sleep in children. Thank you, Pat, for the opportunity to research the effectiveness of the bedtime pass and your ongoing belief in my professional capabilities. Brett, thank you for immersing me in behavioral pediatric sleep medicine and sharing your knowledge and contagious enthusiasm for the field.

CHAPTER 1

Description and Diagnosis

This chapter focuses on the primary sleep disturbances commonly exhibited by children and adolescents. The diagnostic information provided in this chapter is taken from the *Diagnostic and Statistical Manual of Mental Disorders*, Fifth Edition (DSM-5; APA 2013) and the *International Classification of Sleep Disorders*, 2nd Edition (ICSD-2; American Academy of Sleep Medicine 2005). The ICSD-2 is referenced because of its utility in identifying and discriminating dyssomnias in children, which are also recognized by the *International Classification of Diseases*, 10th Revision, Clinical Modifications (National Center for Health Statistics 2010). The childhood diagnostic distinctions are useful in forming clinical conceptualizations and developing treatment intervention protocols. The ICSD-3 (American Academy of Sleep Medicine 2014) eliminated the pediatric insomnia classifications while maintaining the other disorders addressed in this chapter. The ISCD and DSM overlap considerably in the description of diagnostic criteria. The ICSD includes sleep disorders not found in the DSM-5. Those disorders found only in the ICSD are identified.

The importance of sleep is well documented in research and lay literature. Efforts to educate the public about the importance of sleep to our health and well-being have increased in recent decades, yet our society remains largely sleep deprived (National Sleep Foundation 2006). The 24-hour access to nearly every waking activity facilitates chronic sleep deprivation. When faced with a choice between sleep or recreation, sleep or work/academic productivity, sleep or exercise, or sleep or nearly anything else, sleep most often loses. A vast percentage of society seems to think 5 to 7 hours of sleep per night is sufficient. The current recommendation for total sleep time for adolescents and older is 9 hours per night

(Ferber 2006). A recent national survey revealed nearly 32 percent of children are sleep deprived (Smaldone, Honig, and Byrne 2007). The seeming undetectable negative consequences of sleep deprivation foster chronic insufficient total sleep time. The negative consequences of sleep deprivation are undetectable because they are not immediate and most are outside of conscience awareness. And the fatigue people experience during the day is managed with caffeine, energy drinks, and other substances that promote wakefulness.

In addition to voluntary sleep deprivation, sleep disorders impact a significant number of children and adolescents. Research has revealed that 20 to 40 percent of children and adolescents experience some type of sleep disorder during their lifetime (Meltzer and Mindell 2006; Mindell et al. 2006). Sleep disturbances are of concern for numerous reasons. The most obvious are the day-to-day struggles parents, children, and teens experience going to bed, falling asleep, and remaining asleep. Such problems often result in increased conflict between parents and children. Sleep problems frequently result in insufficient total sleep time for children and parents as well as teens. Insufficient total sleep time often results in excessive daytime sleepiness. It also has a negative impact on emotion regulation, behavior regulation, physiological functioning as well as learning, growth, and development (Beebe and Gozal 2002; Dahl 1996; Eliasson, King, and Gould 2002; Mindell and Owens 2003; Randazzo et al. 1998; Wolfson and Carskadon 1998).

The majority of sleep disorders exhibited by children and adolescents can be classified into two categories: dyssomnias and parasomnias. Dyssomnias refer to sleep disturbances that interfere with the onset of sleep, the sleep process itself along with excessive daytime sleepiness. Parasomnias are sleep disturbances that disrupt sleep once sleep onset has occurred. Parasomnias occur in association with sleep and may be abnormal behavioral or physiological events. Parasomnias may occur during sleep in general, in association with specific sleep stages or during sleep–wake transitions. Dyssomnias and parasomnias both often result in poor sleep quality. These disorders may also result in children and adolescents sleeping at inappropriate times of the day and insufficient total sleep time.

Dyssomnias are disturbances that interfere with sleep onset and the sleep process. Dyssomnias discussed in this chapter include the following:

- Insomnia
- Behavioral insomnia of childhood: limit-setting type
- Behavioral insomnia of childhood: sleep onset association type
- Circadian rhythm sleep–wake disorders: delayed sleep phase type
- Breathing-related sleep disorder: Obstructive sleep apnea–hypopnea
- Narcolepsy

Parasomnias are disturbances that disrupt sleep once sleep onset has occurred. Parasomnias discussed in this chapter include the following:

- Sleep terrors
- Sleepwalking
- Sleep talking
- Sleep-related eating
- Nightmare disorder
- Rhythmic movement disorder

Dyssomnias

Insomnia

Insomnia is characterized by difficulty falling asleep, remaining asleep, or the failure to feel rested after sleeping. Diagnostic criteria require the problem to be present for at least 1 month, to cause clinically significant impairment in at least one area of functioning and not be caused by another sleep, medical, or substance-use disorder. The most common complaint of insomnia in my clinical practice has been related to initiating sleep at bedtime or sleep onset latency. Less common though prevalent are complaints related to night wakings and difficulty returning to sleep. Far less common are complaints associated with obtaining a sufficient total sleep time and not feeling rested upon waking.

Insomnia impacts individuals of all ages. For children, insomnia has further been defined as one of three subtypes of behavioral insomnia of childhood described in the following sections. Affecting 20 to 30 percent of children, behavioral insomnia is one of the most common sleep disorders found among children (Mindell 1999). When teens present with insomnia, several factors must be evaluated to determine what else may be contributing to their difficulties falling asleep or maintaining sleep. This content is addressed in Chapter 2. Regardless of the person's age, insomnia is frustrating for parents, children, and teens alike.

Insomnia is about not being able to fall asleep or excessive sleep onset latency. Sleep onset latency is the time between when a child is in bed ready to fall asleep and when the child falls asleep. Difficulty falling asleep is not specifically defined. A general rule of thumb to follow clinically in determining "difficulty" falling asleep is the 30-minute rule. If an individual is falling asleep within 30 minutes of going to bed (lights out, activities ceased, and so on), he or she does not have insomnia of initiating sleep. In my clinical practice, I have learned that the general public is of the opinion that once in bed a person should fall asleep nearly immediately. And if still awake after 5 to 10 minutes, he or she is having trouble falling asleep.

From a physiological perspective, it takes a well-rested body (someone who obtains sufficient total sleep nightly) approximately 20 minutes to achieve sleep onset once the individual has gone to bed. Darkness is a cue to the brain to signal the body to produce melatonin. Melatonin is our natural hormone that promotes sleep onset. This process takes time. The signal must occur. Melatonin must be produced. The body must have time to respond to the effects of melatonin. I often explain to individuals that if sleep onset is occurring within a few minutes, the person is likely sleep deprived. When an individual is awake for more than 30 minutes after he or she has gone to bed, this is considered excessive sleep onset latency.

Lying in bed awake (trying to fall asleep) for more than 30 minutes night-after-night often results in several negative outcomes. A primary negative outcome is the learning history being established that will perpetuate difficulty initiating sleep onset if the insomnia goes untreated. This issue is explained in detail in Chapter 2. Additional negative outcomes may include rumination or worry related to not being able to fall asleep, insufficient total sleep time, and daytime sleepiness.

Behavioral Insomnia of Childhood: Limit-Setting Type

"Behavioral insomnia of childhood: limit-setting type" is recognized by the ICSD-2. This disorder is characterized by the features of insomnia previously described. Most often, children exhibit excessive sleep onset latency at bedtime. Some children also exhibit similar difficulties during night wakings. The defining feature of limit-setting type is the condition under which the child ultimately falls asleep. Diagnostic criteria require that when the child finally falls asleep he or she does so independently, in his or her bed, in a quiet dark room. The limit-setting feature is associated with the behaviors that occur between the time the child has been put to bed (tucked in, gone to bed, and so on) and when he or she falls asleep. Children who exhibit "behavioral insomnia of childhood: limit-setting type" engage in behaviors that are incompatible with sleep onset for an extended period of time. These children typically exhibit numerous, repetitive requests or demands (curtain calls as I refer to them in clinic with parents) after they are in bed for the night. A way to think about this sleep disturbance is the children are pushing the limits to avoid going to bed. However, ultimately they finally fall asleep on their own, in their quiet dark rooms.

The negative consequences of "behavioral insomnia of childhood: limit-setting type" are numerous. Conflict between parents and children and impaired relationships are nearly inevitable. Sleep deprivation is common and is highly associated with poor emotional and behavioral regulation during waking hours. The child's sleep schedule is also often disrupted with sleep occurring at inappropriate or nonpreferred times of day. According to the ICSD, this disorder affects 5 to 10 percent of children.

Behavioral Insomnia of Childhood: Sleep Onset Association Type

"Behavioral insomnia of childhood: sleep onset association type" recognized by the ICSD-2 is also defined by the same criteria as insomnia with an additional defining feature associated with how the child falls asleep. For "behavioral insomnia of childhood: sleep onset association type," the child does not fall asleep independently in bed, in a quiet dark room. The child may start out alone in his or her bed, in a quiet dark room; however, he or she does not fall asleep under those conditions. And attempts to have the child fall asleep under those conditions result in behavior that is incompatible with sleep onset: calling out, coming out, crying, playing, and so on. The defining feature of "behavioral insomnia of childhood: sleep onset association type" is the condition under which the child falls asleep.

Children who exhibit "behavioral insomnia of childhood: sleep onset association type" require specific conditions to fall asleep and are dependent on someone or something else to fall asleep. Their sleep onset is associated with the specific presence of someone or something. In other words, these children do not fall asleep alone, in their beds, in quiet dark rooms. And if the specific conditions of the child's sleep onset association are not present, he or she has significant difficulty falling asleep. Clinically, most often younger children present with needing parental presence to fall asleep. This might look like the parent lying in bed with them or being in their room near their bed. A second and common sleep onset association is having a television on and the child falls asleep while watching a movie or television show. Other common conditions include light, music, and reading. For very young children, sleep onset associations often include rocking and feeding to sleep.

The sleep onset associations established for initiating sleep have significant implications for maintaining sleep. Children with "behavioral insomnia of childhood: sleep onset association type" are at significant risk for extended night wakings because of their inability to achieve sleep onset independently. They tend to experience increased frequency of extended night wakings associated with the typical sleep–wake cycles, resulting in disrupted sleep, poor sleep quality, and often insufficient total sleep time. When a child who meets diagnostic criteria for "behavioral insomnia of childhood: sleep onset association type" wakes in the night, the conditions required for sleep onset at bedtime must be recreated in order for the child to resume sleeping. This often requires parental assistance at the least and more often parental presence. As a result, not only the child's sleep is disrupted, but also the parents' sleep.

The negative consequences are numerous for the child and his or her parents. Parent and child frustration at bedtime is common especially when efforts to have the child fall asleep independently are employed unsuccessfully. This frustration may negatively impact the parent–child relationship, the parents' sense of competence, and result in increased conflict between the parent and child. Older children (school age) may also experience a negative impact on their self-perception due to an inability to fall asleep independently. This process also results in a learning history that serves to maintain the cycle. Insufficient total sleep time and poor sleep quality are realities for both the child and his or her parents. The negative consequences of insufficient total sleep time typically include daytime sleepiness and poor emotional and behavioral regulation for the child and the parent as well as the negative consequences for learning growth and development. According to the ICSD, this disorder affects approximately 15 to 20 percent of children.

Clinically it is helpful to think about children who present with "behavioral insomnia of childhood: sleep onset association type" as unable to fall asleep independently. This conceptualization is discussed in Chapter 2. The third type of behavioral insomnia of childhood recognized by ICSD-2 is "behavioral insomnia of childhood: combined type." This disorder is characterized by the sleep onset association difficulties coupled with bedtime resistance or refusal.

Circadian Rhythm Sleep–Wake Disorder: Delayed Sleep Phase Type

"Circadian rhythm sleep–wake disorder: delayed sleep phase type" is characterized by a consistent and persistent pattern of late sleep onset and late morning awakening times. Individuals who present with sleep phase delay are unable to fall asleep at an earlier time. In addition to this delayed sleep pattern, diagnostic criteria also require clinically significant impairment in functioning and the cause of the disturbance not attributable to another sleep disorder, a medical condition or substance use. Clinically in a pediatric population, this disorder often presents as sleep onset around 3 a.m. with morning awakening 8 to 10 hours later when schedules allow. This disorder is more commonly seen among teens in my clinical practice.

When teens present with delayed sleep phase, they often are struggling to awaken in time for school and subsequently are experiencing problems associated with excessive school tardies or absences. When teens awaken in time for school, it is not uncommon to learn that they are falling asleep in class and experience excessive sleepiness until after their preferred wake time (the time associated with their circadian rhythm). It is common to discover during the clinical interview that teens who present with delayed sleep phase are engaged in behaviors incompatible with sleep onset for hours beyond a typical bedtime of 10 or 11 p.m. These activities often include the use of electronics such as video-gaming systems, cell phones, computers, and televisions. For some teens, the demands of their schedules may also result in a delayed sleep phase. Teens who are involved in extracurricular activities, are employed and experience homework demands of challenging academic schedules often find themselves up until late in the night attempting to keep up with their responsibilities and obligations. This pattern, whether it is the result of recreational activities or an overextended schedule, places the individual at high risk for a circadian rhythm sleep–wake disorder.

Youth who present with delayed sleep phase often experience associated negative consequences. The clinical presentation of youth who experience a delayed phase associated with recreational activities is often complicated by a negative perception of and experiences in the school setting that serve to promote school avoidance. Delayed sleep phase may result in increased conflict between teens and parents associated with struggles to have the teen go to bed earlier and because of concerns related to school attendance and academic performance.

Breathing-Related Sleep Disorder: Obstructive Sleep Apnea–Hypopnea

"Breathing-related sleep disorder: obstructive sleep apnea–hypopnea" is characterized by sleep disruption that leads to excessive sleepiness or insomnia resulting from obstruction of the airway while asleep. According to the DSM-5, this disorder affects 1 to 2 percent of children. Diagnostic criteria require that the sleep disturbance is not attributable to a mental disorder, medical condition, or substance use. Diagnosis of obstructive sleep apnea often includes assessment during an overnight sleep study (polysomnography). This sleep study records the frequency of apneas (the child stops breathing), hypopneas (abnormally slow or shallow breathing), and hypoventilation (abnormal blood oxygen and carbon dioxide levels). When a child exhibits a sufficient number of apnea events that result in insufficient oxygen levels caused by airway obstruction, he or she is diagnosed with obstructive sleep apnea. Children who present with obstructive sleep apnea–hypopnea may also exhibit snoring, labored breathing while asleep, daytime mouth breathing, and unusual postures while sleeping. In children, the most common sources of obstruction are tonsils and adenoids.

As with the other sleep disorders, a breathing-related sleep disorder has serious consequences for the child associated with the depletion of oxygen in the child's bloodstream and impaired quality of sleep. Children may present with attention and learning problems, poor behavioral and emotional regulation, morning headaches, and though less common daytime sleepiness.

Narcolepsy

Narcolepsy is characterized by irresistible attacks of refreshing sleep that occur at least three times per week over the course of three consecutive months. Diagnostic criteria also require the presence of cataplexy (sudden bilateral loss of muscle tone for brief episodes often triggered by intense emotional expression) and/or hypnagogic (dreamlike imagery before falling asleep) or hypnopompic (dreamlike imagery just after awakening) hallucinations or muscle paralysis entering or waking from sleep. The condition may not be attributable to substance use or a medical condition. Diagnosis requires a multiple sleep latency test (MLST). Children who exhibit pathological sleepiness and two or more sleep-onset rapid eye movement (REM) periods (fall directly into REM) sleep during the MLST and do not exhibit the other symptoms are often considered to have narcolepsy. Narcolepsy is more common among adolescents than younger children. It is typically described as irresistible sleep attacks that last for 10 to 20 minutes (although undisturbed the individual may sleep up to an hour) that occur two to six times per day. The individual cannot resist falling asleep regardless of the current activity. The most common and early consequence of narcolepsy is daytime sleepiness.

Parasomnias

Parasomnias are classified in the DSM-5 into two categories: non-rapid eye movement (NREM) sleep arousal disorders and REM sleep behavior disorder. The NREM sleep arousal disorders are discussed in this chapter due to their prevalence among children and adolescents. The NREM sleep arousal disorders typically occur during the first third of the sleep period.

Sleep Terrors

Sleep terrors, also commonly known as night terrors, are a sleep disorder that can affect people of all ages but is most prevalent in young children. Night wakings, including but not limited to sleep terrors, are exhibited by 25 to 50 percent of infants and toddlers over the age of 6 months (Mindell and Owens 2003). The label, sleep terror, reflects the behavioral presentation rather than the actual experience of the child. Sleep terrors are characterized by an abrupt disruption of sleep approximately 3 hours after falling asleep with the child screaming and crying uncontrollably for 1 to 10 minutes. Diagnostic criteria also include a presentation of appearing fearful, autonomic arousal (tachycardia, rapid breathing, sweating, shaking); and unresponsiveness to efforts by others to wake or comfort the child, the absence of a dream and amnesia for the event by the child. The disturbance must cause significant distress or impairment in functioning and may not be attributable to substance use or a medical condition. Sleep terrors are classified as a partial arousal parasomnia. The child seems awake and at the same time is not fully awake, thus partial arousal.

Sleep terrors are frequently disturbing for parents. Parents awaken to their child's screams and crying. Upon seeking out their child, they often find him or her sitting up or flailing about in bed. The child's eyes are often open and seem to look through his or her parents. The child not only sounds terrified (therein lies the name) but also looks terrified as well. The parent's attempts to calm or soothe the child are met with resistance and largely fail. Typically, after a few minutes (what may seem like an eternity to parents) the child lies back down and resumes sleeping peacefully. In the morning, the child has no memory of the event. The parents, on the other hand, remember the seeming fear they observed and heard; must deal with their loss of sleep and recall their failure to soothe the child. The child experiences impaired sleep quality that may have negative consequences for daytime functioning including poor behavioral and emotional regulation and increased fatigue.

Sleepwalking

Sleepwalking, another partial arousal parasomnia common among children, is characterized by getting out of bed and walking (children may also engage in running, jumping, or other movements as well as talking) while still asleep. Diagnostic criteria also include blank stare, unresponsive to others, very difficult to wake, amnesia for the event, and no impairment of mental or behavioral activity within a few minutes of awakening from the event. Additional criteria include: clinically significant distress or impairment in functioning and the sleepwalking is not attributable to substance use or a medical condition.

As with sleep terrors, sleepwalking events typically occur toward the end of the first third of the night's sleep period. A child who exhibits sleepwalking may exhibit complex motor behaviors beyond walking. The child may run through the home, somewhat navigating stairs, doorways, and furniture. Children may urinate while sleepwalking although not necessarily in the bathroom. It is not uncommon for children to urinate in a closet while sleepwalking. Children may also appear to be trying to escape something while they are sleepwalking. Children typically return to bed without fully awakening and resume peaceful sleep. At times, the child may lie down somewhere else in the house and sleep till morning. In the morning, the child has no recall for the event and is surprised to find him or herself sleeping somewhere other than in his or her bed when this occurs.

Sleepwalking may be triggered by internal states such as a full bladder or external stimuli like a noise or the movement of a pet on the bed. Sleepwalking can pose danger for children in various ways. During sleepwalking, children have succeeded in leaving the home. Keep in mind, the child is not awake, he or she is likely not dressed appropriately for the weather and is unresponsive to others around him or her. The child may also injure him or herself bumping into furniture, climbing stairs, or exiting the home by walking out of a window. Sleepwalking results in impaired sleep quality and may result in daytime sleepiness or impaired emotional and behavioral regulation as well.

Sleep Talking

Sleep talking is a partial arousal parasomnia recognized by ICSD. Sleep talking is characterized by talking or uttering sounds aloud during sleep. Sleep talking may occur independently or in conjunction with other sleep disorders including sleepwalking and obstructive sleep apnea. A child may seem to respond to others talking to him or her but the articulation is poor and actual dialogue is absent. Parents who attend to their child during sleep talking may find the child has his or her eyes open and, as with other parasomnias, the child is engaged in a blank stare. Children also demonstrate amnesia for the event. Sleep talking can occur throughout the night's sleep period. Sleep talking may be triggered by internal or external stimuli. Sleep talking may result in impaired quality of sleep for the child and other family members. Furthermore, the child may be embarrassed by the behavior.

Sleep-Related Eating

Sleep-related eating is included as a specifier for sleepwalking in DSM-5 and an independent sleep disorder in ICSD. Sleep-related eating is a partial arousal parasomnia that poses significant challenges to the individuals who experience this sleep disorder. Sleep-related eating is the engagement in eating behavior during arousal from sleep at least one time per week. Amnesia for the event is also a diagnostic criterion. Sleep-related eating differs from nocturnal eating as individuals who exhibit nocturnal eating are fully awake. Evidence of sleep-related eating is typically present in the form of wrappers, partially eaten food, or crumbs upon waking in the morning. Individuals who exhibit sleep-related eating typically eat high-calorie foods and foods not typically eaten by the individual when awake. This sleep disorder poses various risks to people in terms of the types of foods eaten during an episode (e.g., raw bacon) the preparation of food (e.g., cooking, putting jellied bread or raw bacon in a toaster) and the impact on diet, especially for individuals with diabetes or those who are overweight. Sleep-related eating typically presents in adolescence.

Nightmare Disorder

Nightmare disorder differs from the other parasomnias in important ways. First they are more likely to occur in the second half to the last third of the sleep period as compared to the first third. Nightmares are also typically recalled by the child in detail. Nightmare disorder is characterized by detailed recall of extremely frightening dreams that typically threaten ones security or survival. Upon awakening, the child is alert and oriented and the dream itself or awakenings that result cause significant distress or impairment in functioning. The cause may not be attributable to another mental disorder, substance use or medical condition.

Nightmare disorder may impact sleep in several ways. Children who experience nightmares may be fearful of going to sleep and avoid doing so in an attempt to prevent having a nightmare. This strategy typically leads to insufficient total sleep time for children. The awakenings associated with nightmares also have a negative impact on sleep quality resulting from the disruption in sleep and potential reduction in total sleep time for children and parents. Once a child wakes from a nightmare, he or she may have difficulty returning to sleep due to the emotional arousal associated with the nightmare (e.g., fear, anxiety). Such disruption to a child's sleep may negatively impact the child's daytime functioning, resulting in excessive daytime sleepiness, poor behavioral and emotional regulation, poor concentration, anxiety and depression.

Rhythmic Movement Disorder

Rhythmic movement disorder is included in ICSD. It is not included in the DSM-5. Rhythmic movement disorder is most common among infants and young children. It is characterized by the demonstration of repetitive rhythmic movement (e.g., rocking, head banging, swaying) by a child in association with achieving sleep onset. A sleep-related movement disorder impacts approximately 2 to 8 percent of children. Although head banging and other rhythmic movement disorders cause distressing sounds, no reports of serious injury from this disorder have been reported. According to the ICSD, this type of behavior is common in typically developing children demonstrated by approximately 59 percent of 9-month old children. By 18 months, about one-third of children engage in body rocking, head banging, head rolling, and so on. By 5 years of age, just 5 percent of children exhibit such rhythmic body movements. Rhythmic movement disorder is diagnosed only if the movement results in serious injury or interferes with sleep.

Conclusion

Sleep problems are among the most commonly reported medical problems in our society. Yet, in my clinical experience, clinicians do not routinely screen for sleep problems. The implications of impaired sleep resulting in poor sleep quality and/or insufficient total sleep time are broad and significant. Best practice would indicate that assessment and treatment of sleep disorders are fundamental to the treatment of a variety of medical and mental health clinical presentations.

CHAPTER 2

Conceptualization

A consistent and intended message throughout this book is the importance of sleep to healthy development, growth, learning, and day-to-day functioning. Research is clear on the negative effects of sleep deprivation for the human body and our ability to function optimally. Yet, as a society we are sleep deprived. Some people realize they are sleep deprived and long for more sleep or at least imagine getting more sleep. Others are sleep deprived and have no awareness of this fact. Current recommendations for total sleep time indicate 9 hours of sleep nightly for adults. Ask yourself and those around you, "When was the last time you achieved 9 hours of sleep at night?"

Beebe (2011) does an excellent job reviewing the sleep research in children and adolescents. Research has shown that insufficient total sleep time for five (and in some cases even fewer) nights has significantly increased negative ramifications for functioning. Impaired sleep quality, common among children who present with obstructive sleep apnea and/or parasomnias, has also been demonstrated to result in significant negative consequences for children and adolescents. Among children and adolescents, insufficient total sleep time and/or poor sleep quality increase risk for accidental injury, increased risk taking behavior and car accidents, increased susceptibility to illness, memory loss, inattention, impaired learning and poor mood regulation.

There are several factors that likely contribute to the pattern of sleep deprivation present in our society. Data are provided below that illustrate the gradual decline in total sleep time attained on average since the early 1900s.

1910—9.25 hours
1960—8.5 hours
1980—8 hours

2002—7 hours

2013—6.8 hours

A more obvious explanation for the overall decreased total sleep time is the introduction of electricity. The end of daylight is no longer a factor that governs the separation between work or waking day and night or sleep time. In more recent years the advances in electronics and our ever-increasing 24/7, global lifestyle have added to the tendency to prioritize activity over sleep. Light is a key factor in obtaining the sleep we need. Whether it is sunlight, electrical lights, or the light emitted from electronic devices, light promotes wakefulness. The influence of light is important to keep in mind when treating sleep disorders.

Another less obvious factor is a general lack of awareness. This lack of awareness spans simply not knowing how much sleep is recommended as well as how our current functioning is being impacted. In essence, what we do not know, we do not know. If someone is chronically sleep deprived, he or she likely has little to no awareness of what it feels like when sufficient sleep is obtained on a nightly basis night-after-night. We do not know that we might have learned a new skill or solved a recent problem more quickly. We do not realize we might not have caught that most recent virus and several others during the course of the year if we had been well rested. We are able to maintain this less than optimal functioning and combat drowsiness with a variety of aids in the form of pills and drinks that supply caffeine and other chemicals to promote wakefulness and energy.

Children rely on parents to ensure that they are getting an adequate amount of sleep daily. Not only is it important for parents to be informed about recommended total sleep time, but also the importance of setting limits for daytime activities, electronic use, and the sleep environment to promote healthy sleep. Modeling healthy sleep practices is also important. When parents lack information about developing healthy sleep habits, it is unlikely their children will consistently obtain sufficient sleep for optimal health and functioning. When problems arise related to health, mood, growth, attention, and so on, the first reaction is not often one that includes increasing total sleep time on an ongoing basis. Attending to total sleep time is among the important first steps in assessing and treating a variety of childhood and adolescent concerns.

Recommended Total Sleep Time

The recommendations for total sleep time change with age. Recommendations have changed over the years as we learn more about the necessity of sleep to our physical, cognitive, and mental health. In very young children, recommendations include nighttime sleep and daytime sleep or naps. Newborns spend the majority of every 24-hour sleeping, 16 hours on average with a range of 14 to 18 hours. The first year of life marks the sharpest downward trend in total sleep time compared to rest of childhood and adolescence. By 1 year of age, the recommended average total sleep time is 11¾ hours, a decrease of 4¼ hours in 1 year. The decrease in recommended total sleep time becomes much more gradual between 1 and 10 years of age with a total decrease of only 1¾ hours by 10 years of age. The biggest change during this time period is the elimination of napping between 3 and 5 years of age. The elimination of naps results in consolidation of sleep during nighttime hours. The decrease in recommended total sleep time becomes even more gradual between 10 and 17 years of age. At 10 years, the recommended total sleep time is 10 hours. At 17 years of age, it is 9 hours. The recommendation of 9 hours holds for anyone age 17 or older.

Table 2.1 lists the recommended total sleep time from birth through age 17 years. This information is taken from Richard Ferber's book (2006), *Solve Your Child's Sleep Problems*, revised edition.

Sleep Structure

Sleep is a very active process. While sleep is restorative, it is far from a passive process. The body rests while the central nervous system and other major systems, cardiac, respiratory, circulatory, endocrine, work diligently. A few of the numerous critical activities occurring during the various sleep phases include: release of growth hormone, decrease in cortisol secretion, establishment of short-term memories as long-term memories, and strengthening of new cognitive learning and motor skills.

Obtaining a sufficient amount of sleep is critical to ensuring all of the active processes that occur during sleep may be accomplished. The various processes occur during different phases of the sleep cycle. There are two sleep states that are quite different: rapid eye movement (REM)

Table 2.1 Recommended total hours of sleep by age

Age	Total Hours	Range	Day	Number of Naps
1 week	16	14–18	Varied	Varied
1 month	14	12 ½–15 ½	Varied	Varied
3 months	13	12–14	4 ½	3–4
6 months	12 ½	11 ½-13 ½	3 ¼	2–3
9 months	12 ¼	11 ¼–13 ¼	2 ¾	2
12 months	11 ¾	11–12 ½	1 ½–2 ½	1–2
18 months	11 5/8	11–12 ¼	2	1
2 years	11 ½	11–12	1 7/8	1
3 years	11 ¼	10 ¾–11 ¾	0–1 ½	0–1
4 years	11	10 ½–11 ½	0–1	0–1
5 years	10 ¾	10 ¼–11 ¼	0	0
6 years	10 ½	10–11	0	0
7 years	10 3/8	9 7/8–10 7/8	0	0
8 years	10 ¼	9 ¾–10 ¾	0	0
9 years	10 1/8	9 5/8–10 5/8	0	0
10 years	10	9 ½–10 ½	0	0
11 years	9 7/8	9 3/8–10 3/8	0	0
12 years	9 ¾	9 ¼–10 ¼	0	0
13 years	9 5/8	9 1/8–10 1/8	0	0
14 years	9 ½	9–10	0	0
15 years	9 ¼	8 ¾–9 ¾	0	0
16 years	9 1/8	8 5/8–9 5/8	0	0
17 years	9	8 ½–9 ½	0	0

sleep and non-REM sleep. During non-REM sleep, the child lies quietly and restorative processes are active. Dreaming occurs during the REM state along with increased physiological activity. During a night's sleep, children cycle back and forth between REM and non-REM sleep while also experiencing, typically, brief occasional wakings.

Non-REM

Non-REM sleep consists of four sleep stages: Stage I, Stage II, Stage III, and Stage IV. Stage I is the first sleep phase that occurs as children fall asleep. It is a state of drowsiness. Stage I non-REM sleep is considered a transition stage between wakefulness and Stage II non-REM sleep. As children shift from Stage I to Stage II non-REM sleep, brain activity shifts and reveals the introduction of brief episodes of slow wave sleep and brief episodes of very rapid brain wave activity during Stage II non-REM sleep. During Stage II, children are easily awakened and may report they have not yet slept. Stage II is followed by Stages III and IV delta or deep sleep. These two stages are very similar and brain wave activity is dominated by slow "delta" waves. The child's heart rate becomes regular and he or she is very difficult to wake.

REM

During non-REM sleep children are able to move. During REM sleep children are unable to move, as nerve impulses from the brain to the muscles are blocked. The exceptions include the eyes, respiration, and hearing. As a result, children are effectively paralyzed during REM sleep. This process prevents children from acting out their dreams. Other physiological changes that occur during REM sleep include: irregular breathing and heart rate, increased oxygen use, increased blood flow to the brain along with increased brain temperature, and more active brain wave patterns. Changes in kidney function, reflexes, and hormone release also occur during REM sleep.

Beginning at approximately 3 months of age, the first third and the last hour or two of sleep are spent in delta or Stage IV non-REM sleep. During the hours in between, children cycle between brief periods of wakefulness, light non-REM sleep and REM sleep. As children age and the total sleep time needed decreases, the time spent in each sleep state decreases. The length of the sleep cycle (the time between falling asleep

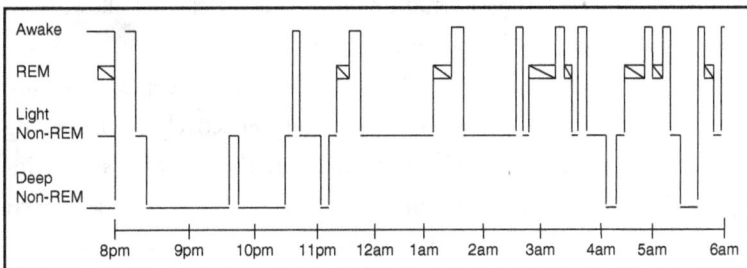

Figure 2.1 Typical sleep stages in young children

and the first brief awakening) increases from approximately 50 minutes in children to 90 minutes in adolescents. While the time spent in Stage IV delta sleep decreases from childhood to adolescence, this stage still accounts for a quarter of the total nightly sleep period. Figure 2.1 depicts the typical sleep cycles for a young child (Ferber 2006, p. 25).

The Sleep–Wake Cycle

Two biological processes control the sleep–wake cycle: homeostatic sleep drive and circadian system or rhythm. The homeostatic sleep drive is the body's increased pressure to sleep in response to being awake over time. The circadian rhythm refers to the central nervous system's governance over wakefulness and sleepiness at different times during the 24-hour day.

Circadian Rhythm

Circadian refers to a 24-hour cycle. In humans, the circadian rhythm is the 24-hour cycle or rhythm that governs wakefulness, appetite, hormone secretions, and many other physiological functions. The circadian drive is responsible for increasing wakefulness during the day and sleepiness through the night. In humans, the circadian cycle runs slightly slower than 24 hours. We are able to "reset" the circadian system each day through exposure to light. The ability to reset also explains how we are able to adjust to different time zones when we travel. The circadian system also accounts for how we are able to pull an "all-nighter" and function somewhat adequately the next day. When we stay up all night, we resist the drive to sleep while the circadian system continues through its cycle. With morning comes the wakefulness phase of the cycle that allows us to remain awake and alert throughout the day.

The circadian system also explains the difficulties people who work the third shift experience. We are not able to effectively shift sleeping hours alone and maintain optimal functioning. The circadian system integrates all of our biological systems to work in concert within the context of our physical environment governed by day and night. When we travel to another time zone half-way around the world, it takes some time to adjust and we can adjust. We have light on our side. When we attempt to change our schedule and make night our day and day our night, this proves much more challenging. When the circadian system is challenged by travel, night shift hours, or staying up all night and day repeatedly, the body and the person suffer. The various physiological systems get out of sync, you do not feel well during the day, and your ability to think, reason, or learn is impaired.

Homeostatic Drive

The homeostatic drive works in opposition to the circadian system. The homeostatic drive is responsible for increased sleepiness, the longer we are awake and decreased sleepiness the longer we are asleep. Without the circadian system, we would be falling asleep in the early evening hours and waking up in the early morning hours. After being awake long enough, we would fall asleep. After sleeping long enough, we would wake up. It may seem like this is what happens; however, it is not. If the homeostatic drive was working in isolation, we would get and feel increasingly sleepy as the day progressed. We would struggle to remain awake in the evening hours, and participating in evening activities would be challenging due to sleepiness on a daily basis. As it is, we remain awake and alert until our circadian system and homeostatic drive work together resulting in falling asleep. The homeostatic drive and the circadian system align at night to promote sleep. The circadian system also allows us to remain asleep even though the homeostatic drive for sleep decreases the longer we sleep. The two systems working together allow us to achieve the amount of sleep we need that is critical to our healthy functioning.

Specific Sleep Disorders

Insomnia

An important concept central to understanding sleep disorders characterized by insomnia is the fact that falling asleep is a learned behavior. We are not born knowing how to fall asleep. We learn how to fall asleep. From birth, infants need help or assistance to fall asleep. This is no different from the help they need to access food, diaper changes, getting dressed, ambulating, and so much more. When it comes to sleep, the assistance infants need involves decreased stimulation in terms of noise, light, and interaction. That is, they need an environment that is conducive to sleeping.

Insomnia may occur for a variety of reasons. The development of behavioral insomnia of childhood is explained next. However, attempting to adjust bedtime to occur earlier or inadvertently or intentionally changing the sleep environment or other external factors may result in insomnia. Making radical adjustments in bedtime schedules without attending to a variety of other factors will very likely work against your biological systems, the homeostatic and circadian drive. Changing the sleep environment will work against the individual's learning history. If light is introduced via electronics, this will work against the person's biological systems. Illness, stress, variable work schedules, travel, fear, depression, and many other factors may all result in or increase risk for insomnia as well. Staying up late several nights in a row out of necessity or want makes it difficult to return to a previously established earlier bedtime.

When concerns for insomnia are related to maintaining sleep, that is, extended night wakings, two key variables are considered. One variable to consider is related to the child or adolescent's sleep onset associations. Sleep onset associations are discussed next. When the child's or adolescent falls asleep alone in a quiet dark room, another important variable to consider is the amount of time the child or adolescent spends in bed. When a child or adolescent is in bed beyond the number of hours required to obtain the recommended total sleep time, he or she is at risk for extended nighttime wakings. I explain to parents that the child (this is most often the case) is achieving the recommended total sleep time (say 10 hours) and because he or she is in bed longer than that (say 12 hours), the child is putting waking time in the middle of the night. I further explain that the total sleep time is adequate (when it is); however, the child's sleep quality is impaired by the shortened sleep periods and night wakings.

Behavioral Insomnia of Childhood: Sleep Onset Association Type

For many young children falling asleep co-occurs with feeding, nursing, rocking, swaying, singing, riding in a car, sitting in a car seat, lying next to a parent, sucking on a pacifier, light, music, a movie or television show playing or any one of a host of possibilities. As children age, parents increasingly want and expect their child to fall asleep independently. In an effort to achieve this end parents change their bedtime routine, placing their child in bed and leaving the room with an instruction to the child to stay in bed and go to sleep. The child fails to fall asleep and begins to engage in behavior incompatible with falling asleep. The child is truly not to blame. No one is to blame. The fact is these children do not know how to fall asleep alone in a quiet dark room. They have not yet *learned* how to fall asleep alone in a quiet dark room. They have learned to fall asleep with a parent present or some other specific set of conditions.

In this situation, the child experiences insomnia until the conditions necessary for sleep onset are met. Once the conditions are met, the child typically falls asleep quickly. In my clinical practice, children and teens present with sleep onset association problems. It seems parents most often seek clinical services for their children around the ages of 2 years or 10 years. At 2 years of age, parents are often assisting their children in falling asleep in their own beds. At 10 years of age, parents are seeking assistance in transitioning from co-sleeping to having their child sleep in his or her own bed. Regardless of age, parental presence has been the most common problematic sleep onset association reported by parents in my clinical practice.

Behavioral Insomnia of Childhood: Limit-Setting Type

Children who exhibit "behavioral insomnia of childhood: limit-setting type" have a different learning history associated with falling asleep. These children ultimately fall asleep alone in their own bed in a quiet dark room. These children typically engage in numerous repeated acts of calling out for their parents, coming out of their rooms and/or playing in their rooms before finally falling asleep. They may engage in these behaviors for one or more hours resulting in an excessive sleep onset latency or insomnia.

Children who exhibit "behavioral insomnia of childhood: limit-setting type" actively resist going to sleep rather than exhibit an inability to fall asleep independently. When examined from a behavioral perspective, this resistance serves an escape or avoidance function. The process of going to bed and falling asleep is similar to time out. The child is no longer engaged in the activities of the day even though other family members remain active. The child is expected to lie in bed, in a quiet dark room, doing nothing, and to fall asleep. This set of expectations competes with far more reinforcing stimuli including: parental attention, physical activity (getting a drink, going potty, getting a hug), playing with toys, watching television, reading books, among a plethora of other options. In addition to resisting falling asleep, children learn to pair going to bed with making these numerous requests and attempts to remain awake. This combination makes it difficult for children to fall asleep readily once placed in bed without direct intervention.

Rhythmic Movement Disorder

Rhythmic movement disorder is similar conceptually to a sleep onset association disorder. That is, the child learns to fall asleep while engaging in a rhythmic movement. Over time, this pattern of falling asleep is essentially established as a habit. A learned behavior, a new pattern of falling asleep can be established. An incompatible behavior must be identified and reinforced while the ability and opportunity to engage in the rhythmic movement behavior are prevented.

Delayed Sleep Phase

Delayed sleep phase results from a shift in the circadian rhythm. This occurs over time when sleep onset occurs consistently much later than a typical bedtime. More common in teens, this delay may result from engagement in preferred activities until late in the night; avoiding bedtime for hours due to fears or other anxiety disorders; or needing to stay up late to meet obligations related to home, school, or work. Each of these paths may lead to a pattern of sleep onset that occurs after 2 a.m. For teens who present with sleep phase delay, going to bed earlier results in lying awake until the time they typically fall asleep. Their circadian rhythm has shifted and treatment requires shifting it again to establish the preferred sleep schedule.

Anxiety and Sleep

Another common source of insomnia is worry or rumination. Children who experience impairing anxiety may experience interference with sleep onset. Some children experience fears associated with being in a quiet dark room alone. Other children ruminate or worry about events of the day or anticipated events scheduled. Lying in bed in a quiet dark room removed from the activities and distractions of the day is fertile ground for fearful thoughts. Rumination may result in children resisting bedtime and typically interferes with engaging in behaviors that are compatible with sleep onset.

Children who exhibit separation anxiety disorder may struggle to fall asleep due to separation from their parents. Their fears associated with separation may make it difficult to relax, self-regulate, and fall asleep.

Children who exhibit obsessive compulsive disorder may display symptoms that interfere with sleep onset. Contamination fears may result in excessive showering, washing rituals and/or laundering of sheets that preclude getting into bed. Or such fears may result in a compulsion that requires getting back out of bed such as rituals related to locking and checking windows and doors. Fears of intruders often impact sleep onset as well. Obsessions and compulsions can delay bedtime, interfere with sleep onset, and reduce total sleep time.

Parasomnias

The exact cause of parasomnias is yet to be determined. We do know there are neurological factors, genetic factors, and environmental factors. We also know parasomnia events are more likely to occur during the first third of the sleep period. This section focuses on the environmental and physiological factors that seem to increase the likelihood of children exhibiting parasomnias. That being said, clinical interviews often reveal that children who exhibit parasomnias have parents who as children or adults exhibited parasomnias (a genetic factor).

The frequency or occurrence of parasomnia events increases when children experience insufficient total sleep time or impaired sleep quality (an environmental factor). In other words, the child is sleep deprived in terms of total sleep time and/or uninterrupted sleep.

One way to conceptualize parasomnias is to think about them as a struggle between what the body wants and the circadian rhythm cycle. For children who are sleep deprived, the body wants more stage IV or delta sleep and the circadian rhythm says it is time to transition into lighter sleep. When this happens, the child gets caught in the transition resulting in a partial arousal parasomnia. The child is moving to a lighter stage of sleep and is unable to do so smoothly due to the pressure resulting from sleep deprivation for more delta sleep.

When parasomnia events occur, children engage in activities associated with being awake, crying, talking, walking, running, eating, and more. The child may look at the parent and may even respond to the parent verbally. This can make it difficult to determine if the child is awake. When children are inconsolable, nonresponsive or resistant to a parent's efforts to interact or redirect them it seems more clear that they are experiencing a parasomnia event. In both circumstances, parents typically report that the child did not really seem to be fully awake. In the morning, the child has no recall for the event. This amnesia further confirms that it was a parasomnia event.

The timing of the event also matters. If you recall from the section on sleep phases in this chapter, Stages III and IV non-REM sleep occur predominantly during the first third of the sleep period followed by a transition to a lighter sleep stage or brief awakening. In clinic, when parents report their child is having bad dreams and they describe inconsolable crying, screaming, and so on within 1 to 4 hours of sleep onset, it is highly unlikely that dreaming has occurred. Dreaming does not occur during non-REM sleep. It may seem as though the child is reacting to a bad dream, especially when night terrors are exhibited. The child appears fearful and distraught and may thrash about in his or her bed. Not only is the child in a non-REM sleep phase, you may also recall that children and adolescents (and adults for that matter) experience muscle paralysis during REM sleep. That means they cannot move while they are dreaming. They may appear to be dreaming even though they are not dreaming. So the timing of as well as the behavior exhibited during a parasomnia event point to a non-REM sleep state. More specifically, such events point to the transition from the delta sleep phase to a lighter non-REM sleep phase.

Conclusion

All of this information is important to keep in mind as you evaluate and assess the sleep habits and patterns of children and adolescents. Sleep matters to overall health and functioning. Including exploration of sleep in initial and ongoing assessment is important. When disrupted or disordered sleep is of concern, gathering comprehensive and detailed information about current and recent past sleep behavior is essential. This information will allow you to develop a clear understanding of the child or adolescent's current sleep behavior, determine if he or she meets diagnostic criteria for a sleep disorder and formulate an effective treatment protocol. The evaluation and assessment of sleep are addressed in the next chapter. Treatment is addressed in Chapter 4.

CHAPTER 3

Evaluation and Assessment

The importance of sleep to the health and well-being of every child and adolescent cannot be overstated. Sleep matters. Getting enough sleep. Getting quality sleep. Sleeping at the appropriate time of day consistent with our circadian cycle. It all matters. Responsible, effective clinical practice includes attending to sleep for every client regardless of the presenting concern. Attending to sleep may reveal healthy sleep habits and adequate total sleep time. When this occurs, clinicians are encouraged to commend the clients (and their parents) for this accomplishment. It is also a great opportunity to share with them how much sleep is recommended for the client's age and that of any other children and the parents in the household. Psychoeducation on recommended total sleep time is a first step in achieving adequate sleep.

This chapter covers the basic strategies clinicians may employ in evaluating and assessing sleep in an outpatient treatment setting. It does not include information specific to conducting overnight sleep studies or nocturnal polysomnography (PSG); the assessment required for diagnosis of a variety of sleep disorders including: obstructive or central sleep apnea and narcolepsy. Information regarding when a clinician is encouraged to refer a client for an overnight sleep study is addressed in Chapter 4. This chapter includes discussion of conducting the clinical interview, utilization of a sleep diary, and standardized sleep scales.

Clinical Interview

It is important to ask every client about his or her sleep. Sleep concerns are not typically brought up unless they are the concerns that prompted seeking outpatient services. Simply asking about sleep concerns is minimally effective. If you recall from the previous chapters, people in general are ill informed regarding the total sleep time recommended for children (and adults) of all ages. It is incumbent on the clinician to explore sleep, briefly screening key details to determine if further assessment is warranted. It is highly likely that sleep hygiene as well as total sleep time concerns will be exposed. When initial screening questions reveal concerns, more detailed evaluation is recommended.

Clinicians are encouraged to build questions about sleep into the standard intake interview. At what point in the interview sleep is assessed matters little if at all. The key is to make sure sleep is assessed. For very young children, you will direct your questions to the parents. When you are working with a school-age child, I recommend asking the child as well as his or her parents about the child's sleep habits. This allows you to iden- tify the discrepancies and may indicate the need for further assessment. When working with adolescents, I focus my questions on the adolescent. I make sure to ask the parents if they share the same perspective as the adolescent, again looking for discrepancies. In my clinical practice, school-age children tend to exaggerate sleep difficulties while adolescents under report. The exaggeration by school-age children is likely reflective of their skills for estimating time and objective recall rather than inten- tional misrepresentation. It is my experience that adolescents are reluctant to report just how late they stay up and how little sleep they are obtaining. I attempt to convey the importance of accurate reporting in order to help them effectively. Parents tend to "call out" their teens when the teens' report is in question.

A helpful place to start is to simply let the client know you are going to review current sleep practices. I ask about bedtime, morning wake time, napping, falling asleep, and daytime sleepiness. I typically ask the following questions in the order listed.

1. What time do you go to bed?
2. How long does it take you to fall asleep?
3. Once asleep, do you sleep through the night?
4. What time do you get up in the morning?
5. Are you tired during the day?
6. Do you nap during the day?

If any of these questions suggest sleep-related difficulties such as excessive sleep onset latency, frequent night wakings, excessive daytime sleepiness and/or insufficient total sleep time, I recommend following up with more detailed questions as described below. When this information is obtained in the intake interview, there may not be sufficient time to conduct a more in-depth interview. I typically convey my impression that sleep may be of concern and encourage the client and his or her parents to consider addressing sleep more directly. When they agree, I provide them with a sleep diary to be completed prior to the next appointment. I then conduct the detailed sleep interview at the next appointment when the sleep diary has been returned.

When a client presents to clinic specifically for sleep concerns, a completed sleep diary (discussed later in this chapter) is required for the intake interview. My practice is to conduct the interview as described below, before reviewing the sleep diary. I am very interested in the client's perception of his or her sleep as provided via the interview. The extent to which the client's verbal report matches the sleep diary is clinically useful information. One example of this utility is when a client reports excessive sleep onset latency and the clinical interview and sleep diary reveal ready sleep onset. In this situation, psychoeducation regarding healthy sleep onset latency is important and may alleviate the client's frustration.

When a client presents to clinic for sleep concerns or the screening questions above suggest sleep concerns, I conduct a sleep interview. This interview is a more detailed look at a client's sleep-related practices. I typically begin by having the client or parents describe the bedtime routine. I ask the client to include anchors in terms of time as the routine is described. This approach allows me to attend to factors related to the client's sleep hygiene. You might recall from Chapter 2 that falling asleep is a learned behavior. Exploration of sleep hygiene helps you identify factors that may impede the child's ability to fall asleep when desired or how desired. This information also lets you know if the current routine could lead to problems even if there are no current complaints related to the routine.

There are a number of factors of interest when assessing sleep hygiene via a description of the bedtime routine. You are looking for practices that work against readily falling asleep alone in a quiet dark room. The keywords in that sentence are "readily," "alone," "quiet," and "dark." In reality, there are many ways the bedtime routine can affect the ability of a child or adolescent to accomplish this task. The first determination is whether or not a bedtime routine is in place. If the child gets ready for bed randomly from one day to the next and falls asleep spontaneously on the floor, couch, or chair in the midst of another activity like watching TV or playing, he or she does not have a consistent bedtime routine. In situations like this, the child has limited opportunities to develop healthy paired associations between cues and sleep onset. Said another way, stimulus control for bedtime and sleep is lacking. Most problematic is the reality that the child's bed is not being established as a cue (or stimulus) for sleep onset. As a result, efforts to spontaneously place the child in bed to go to sleep while awake will likely result in bedtime resistance. When the child is placed in bed after falling asleep, you can anticipate problems associated with night wakings.

A healthy or sleep-promoting bedtime routine includes activities that help the child and adolescent discriminate that daytime activities are complete and it is time to go to sleep. Such routines include tasks such as bathing, brushing teeth, going potty, putting on pajamas, bedtime prayers, and hugs and kisses good night. These tasks can typically be accomplished in 20 to 30 minutes. In my clinical practice, bedtime routines derail the learning or pairing of cues that bedtime and sleep are imminent in several ways. Most common is the inclusion of daytime activities after the child is ready for bed, that is, in pajamas and the rest of the routine complete. Frequently described activities include eating a snack, watching TV, reading books, and playing with toys. It is also critical to assess where such activities are occurring. In my clinical practice, such activities most often occur in the child's bed or bedroom. When such activities occur in the child's bed, the strength of the bed as a cue for sleep is diminished.

Another detail to attend to is the changing of clothes into pajamas. The term pajamas is used because of familiarity and for efficiency. It is not necessary for a child to sleep in pajamas specifically. It is important that the child or adolescent sleep in clothes reserved for sleep. Some children and adolescents sleep in the clothes they wore that day or plan to wear the next day. In either case, the clothes do not signal it is time to sleep, an important function of pajamas (stimulus control). The timing of putting on pajamas matters as well. The closer in proximity to the child's bedtime pajamas are put on, the less likely they will be worn during daytime activities, thus strengthening their association with sleep.

In gathering a detailed description of the bedtime routine, you are assessing the extent to which it cues the child or adolescent that it is time to go to bed and sleep. The bedtime routine culminates when the child is told "good night." Once you have a detailed description of the bedtime routine, it is important to assess the sleep environment in detail. It is important to ask for a description of the environment when the child is put to bed. Important aspects of this description include: finding out how much and what sources of light are present, what sounds are present, who is present, what specific objects the child is tucked into bed with, and what the child is doing when he or she falls asleep.

In obtaining this information, you are again looking for practices that interfere with learning to readily fall asleep alone in a quiet dark room. Many aspects of the sleep environment can interfere with developing or learning healthy independent sleep onset skills. The room may allow exposure to too much light. If there is enough light to read a book by, there is too much light. Another source of problematic light is electronic screens. Electronics emit the exact light wavelength that interferes with the production of melatonin, thereby interfering with falling asleep. The light in the child's room might be intentional or it might occur environmentally via street lights or the sun.

Sound is another potential concern for healthy sleep habits and quality nighttime sleep. White noise is acceptable and even recommended. Any other sound may interfere with sleep onset and/or establish an unwanted sleep onset association. Sounds other than white noise also stimulate the brain during sleep, interfering with the brain's ability to accomplish the tasks to be accomplished during sleep. Sounds might include turning on music or a TV to fall asleep by or environmental sounds like train whistles.

For children and adolescents who present to the clinic for sleep concerns, being in bed most often does not result in ready sleep onset. The opposite is often true. The child remains awake for an extended period of time. It is important to obtain a description of what the child does during the time between when he or she is put to bed (or goes to bed) and when he or she falls asleep. The possibilities are numerous. The child might lie in bed quietly. The child might be in and out of bed repeatedly making numerous requests. I refer to this behavior as "curtain calls." The child might call out from his or her bed repeatedly. More curtain calls. The child might get out of bed and play or bring toys into bed and play. The child might be on an electronic device texting, talking, internet surfing, watching videos, and so on. The child might worry about events of the day, anticipated events of tomorrow, or other fears. The child might read or do homework. As this description is obtained, clarifying where the child is doing whatever he or she is doing is important. You want to know what is happening in the bed.

Once you have a handle on the routine and typical bedtime behaviors, you are ready to find out just how the child falls asleep. I typically ask what is happening when the child falls asleep. I ask whether the child is alone or if someone is present. Are sources of sound and light turned off or do they remain on? Does the child fall asleep lying in bed or somewhere else? I also ask about transition objects like special blankets, pacifiers, bottles, or stuffed animals. A clear picture of the behaviors exhibited during sleep onset latency and the conditions at the time of sleep onset are essential to accurate diagnosis and effective treatment planning.

Once you have a clear picture of the bedtime routine, the sleep environment and sleep onset information about night wakings is gathered. If the child sleeps through the night, this is a very brief conversation. For those children who wake in the night, it is important to ask about what time night wakings typically occur, how long the child remains awake, what the child does upon awaking, and what it takes for the child to fall back asleep. Asking about snoring, sleepwalking, sleep talking, sleep-related eating, and bad dreams or nightmares is also important. When asking about snoring, if the child snores you can assess the severity of snoring by asking if snoring can be heard from another room with the door closed. It is also helpful to ask if snoring occurs routinely (most nights) or seems to coincide with colds or allergies. Asking about the child's presentation during night wakings helps you discriminate whether or not the child is exhibiting a partial arousal parasomnia. Asking the parent if the child seems awake and asking the child if he or she remembers the event in the morning helps clarify what is likely happening.

Next you are gathering information about morning wake times and daytime sleepiness. Asking about the time the child or adolescent is awakened, gets out of bed and if the child or adolescent wakes spontaneously are important questions. Talking about napping, what time the child goes down for naps, how long naps last and what it takes to get the child to fall asleep for naps is information you will want to gather. For children beyond napping age, it is important to ask about daytime sleepiness and napping. It is useful to ask about falling asleep in the car, on the bus, and in school specifically when assessing napping with older youth.

Gathering information about a couple of other key daytime behaviors is also important. Caffeine intake, exercise habits, and electronic use are relevant to sleep. Caffeine intake may be more obvious. It is important to ask about the quantity of caffeine intake and how late in the day caffeine is consumed. The timing of exercise matters as well. Clinicians are encouraged to find out when exercise occurs. When and how much time children and adolescents are engaged in electronic use, video games, social media, or texting are relevant to achieving healthy sleep.

Sleep Diary

Once a detailed sleep interview is conducted, it is equally important to consider the information provided by a completed sleep diary (Figure 3.1). For clients who present to the clinic specifically for sleep concerns, the sleep diary is completed prior to the intake appointment. This data is then available for review at the intake appointment. When the brief screening of sleep indicates potential sleep concerns, a sleep diary is provided for completion prior to the next appointment to conduct further assessment. When sleep is not the presenting concern and the screening questions reveal potential concerns, I conduct the more detailed sleep interview at the follow-up appointment when the completed sleep diary is also available. It is my standard practice to require a completed sleep diary before making recommendations regarding sleep difficulties. The sleep diary provides concrete baseline

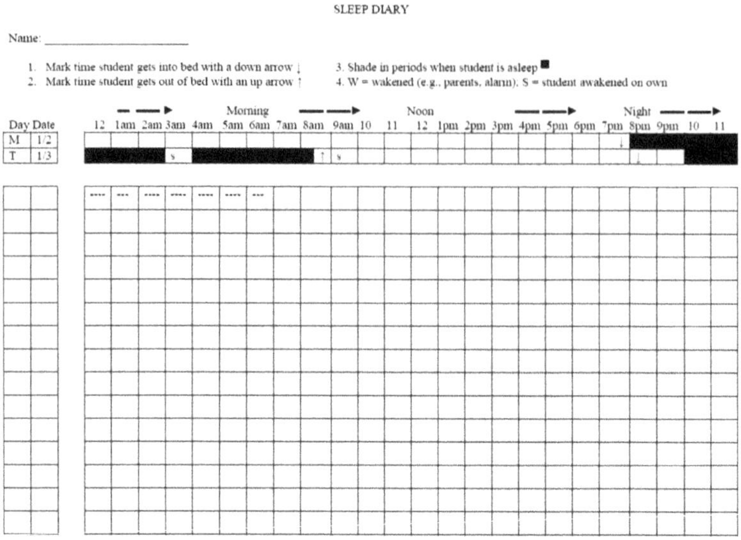

Figure 3.1 Sleep diary

data, highlights specific risk factors for sleep problems, and allows for ongoing progress monitoring. Although the detailed sleep interview is important and useful, it is not sufficient. Verbal reports tend to result in information that focuses on the most severe problems or most recent sleep experiences. The sleep diary helps the clinician assess the severity and stability of the sleep problems described along with numerous other key factors.

When providing clients with a sleep dairy in the intake session for completion prior to the next appointment, it is my practice to fill out the diary for the previous night's sleep with the client. This helps facilitate accurate completion of the diary. When providing the diary prior to the initial intake appointment, I describe how to fill the diary out briefly, inform the client instructions are on the diary, and invite questions should they have any. I make sure to point out the down arrow is used to indicate when the child went to bed and shading begins when sleep onset occurs. I also encourage clients to fill out the diary daily in order to get the most accurate information.

The sleep diary provides an invaluable and comprehensive picture of the child's sleep–wake pattern. As I review the diary, I make sure to confirm that the diary represents typical sleep–wake behavior for the child or adolescent. The completed sleep diary allows the clinician to assess the following factors:

- Bedtime
  - Time in bed at night
  - Time of sleep onset
  - Sleep onset latency
- Nighttime sleep interruptions
  - Time of wakings
  - Number of wakings
  - Duration of wakings
- Morning wake time
- Total time in bed at night
- Average total sleep time at night
- Sleep efficiency
- Naptime
  - Time in bed for naps
  - Time of sleep onset
  - Sleep onset latency
  - Duration of naps
- Average total sleep time in 24 hours
- Consistency in sleep–wake schedule
  - Bedtime
  - Sleep onset
  - Night wakings
  - Morning wake time
  - Naptime
  - Nap duration

When filled out correctly, the sleep diary contains a down arrow that indicates when the child was put in bed for the night. This does not mean the child stayed in bed. Rather it represents when the child or adolescent went to bed or was put to bed with the expectation or hope that he or she would stay in bed. Looking at the sleep diary, the clinician can evaluate how consistent the down arrow is night-to-night and how well it matches the information gathered during the clinical interview. Similarly, the sleep diary clearly depicts sleep onset via shading that begins at the time of sleep onset. Sleep is depicted with shading whereas being awake is depicted by the absence of shading. This allows a clinician to determine what time the child or adolescent actually falls asleep night-to-night and how consistent sleep onset occurs night-to-night.

Similarly the frequency, duration, timing, and consistency of night wakings are also delineated on the diary. Morning wake time is depicted by an up arrow and an "S" or a "W." The S indicates the child woke spontaneously. The W indicates the child was awakened by someone or something (an alarm). All sleep that occurs in every 24-hour period is to be recorded on the diary. This allows the clinician to assess daytime sleep habits as well including: frequency, duration, timing, and consistency of napping.

In addition to revealing sleep–wake patterns, the sleep diary is particularly useful in calculating sleep onset latency, average total nighttime sleep, total time in bed at night, sleep efficiency, average nap duration, and average total sleep time in 24 hours. Each box on the sleep diary represents 1 hour, and boxes are shaded to correspond with the time of sleep onset or awakenings. Thus, a partially shaded box represents the portion of the hour the child was asleep versus awake. Average sleep onset latency is calculated by adding up the nightly sleep onset latencies and dividing the total by the number of nights assessed. The sleep onset latency is the time delineated between the down arrow and when sleep onset occurs as evidenced by the start of shading.

Average total nighttime sleep is calculated by counting the number of hours of sleep each night, adding up the hours and dividing the total by the number of nights assessed. In calculating average nighttime sleep, it is important to only count actual sleep time. This calculation requires excluding any hours or minutes the child was awake in the calculation. Total time in bed is calculated by counting the number of hours between the down arrow depicting bedtime and the up arrow depicting morning wake time for each night. You then add these hours together and divide by the number of nights assessed. Sleep efficiency is calculated by dividing the average number of hours of sleep at night by the average number of hours in bed and multiplying by 100. For example, if a child averages 8 hours of sleep and is in bed for 10 hours his sleep efficiency is 80%.

The total 24-hour sleep time average requires calculation of daytime sleep. The duration of naps is recorded for each day, then added together and finally the total is divided by the number of days assessed. The average nighttime sleep and daytime sleep are then added together to obtain the average total 24-hour sleep time. These calculations allow the clinician to determine if the child is achieving insufficient total sleep time, spending too much time in bed, and or experiencing excessive sleep onset latency.

Specialty Assessments

Clinicians are able to obtain a significant amount of information from the detailed clinical sleep interview and a completed sleep diary. This information is often sufficient in determining a clinical diagnosis and establishing an effective treatment plan. In some instances, additional evaluation is of utility if not necessary. Such evaluation may include standardized rating scales, referral for an overnight PSG, or referral to medical specialists such as an ear, nose, and throat (ENT) physician. Referrals for further medical evaluation are recommended when a clinician suspects sleep apnea, narcolepsy, or seizures during sleep. Children and adolescents who present with loud snoring, daytime sleepiness, and sufficient total sleep time should be considered for referral to a medical specialist. The combination of snoring, sleepiness and sufficient total sleep time suggests that the quality of sleep is impaired, and this could be due to airway obstruction or other medical condition. It is good clinical practice to recommend further evaluation by the primary care physician or an ENT.

For those children or adolescents whom a clinician suspects narcolepsy, further assessment via PSG is required. Children and adolescents who obtain a sufficient amount of total sleep time, do not present with concerns for sleep quality and fall asleep frequently throughout the day may present with narcolepsy. A multiple sleep latency test (MSLT) is required to document both ready onset of sleep and rapid entrance into rapid eye movement (REM) sleep multiple times during daytime hours. Similarly if nighttime seizures are suspected, PSG is required to detect seizure activity.

A number of sleep-related assessment tools are available for clinician use. The tools fall into five categories in terms of assessment including: sleep initiation and maintenance, daytime sleepiness, sleep habits and sleep hygiene, cognitions or beliefs about sleep and multidimensional measures. There are measures available to assess sleep-related concerns for infants through adolescence. Most instruments focus on a particular age range such as infancy, toddlers, school age, and adolescents. A few instruments span early childhood through 18 years of age.

One of the most widely used instruments is the Children's Sleep Habits Questionnaire (CSHQ) by Owens and colleagues (2000). The CSHQ is a multidimensional 35-item questionnaire completed by parents to assess for behavioral and medical sleep problems for children 4 to 10 years of age. A common daytime sleepiness scale is the Epworth Sleepiness Scale (Melendres et al. 2004). This scale was revised for children and includes eight items to assess how likely a child or adolescent is to fall asleep during daytime activities.

A structured clinical interview tool, the B.E.A.R.S. (Owens & Dalzell 2005) aids clinicians in assessing for **b**edtime issues, **e**xcessive daytime somnolence, **n**ight awakenings, **r**egularity and duration of sleep and **s**noring. In 2011, two review articles of pediatric sleep questionnaires were published. These articles investigate the diagnostic utility of the instruments (Spruyt and Gozal 2011) and the psychometric properties of a number of sleep measures (Lewandowski, Toliver-Sokol, and Palermo 2011).

Another device utilized in sleep medicine is the actigraph. An actigraph is a watchlike device that a child or adolescent typically wears on his or her wrist to monitor movement and exposure to light. Similar to activity devices that are popular today, the actigraph records movement as wakefulness and the absence of movement as sleep. Actigraphs can record data up to several weeks at a time and are much more sensitive than activity devices. Although useful, actigraphs have limitations including their cost, inability to distinguish lying still from sleeping, movement disorders from wakefulness, and to differentiate sleep stages. Completion of a sleep diary is recommended when actigraphs are utilized to facilitate interpretation of actigraphy data.

Conclusion

The importance of assessing sleep cannot be overstated. Simply asking if a child or adolescent has any concerns about his or her sleep is inadequate. At the very least, asking a few questions to assess whether or not the child or adolescent is obtaining sufficient total sleep time, having difficulty falling asleep or remaining asleep and/or feels sleepy during the day is responsible clinical practice. When such questions point to sleep concerns, informing children, teens, and parents of the clinical utility of addressing the sleep concerns is best practice. In some cases, sleep will be addressed as a clinical priority. In other situations, sleep will be a secondary or tertiary clinical focus. Clinicians work with children, teens, and parents to determine the best course of treatment in terms of clinical focus and recommended interventions.

CHAPTER 4

Treatment

A variety of interventions are available for the treatment of sleep disorders in children and adolescents. A comprehensive assessment is fundamental to developing an effective treatment protocol. A thorough treatment plan results in successful and efficient outcomes. Overlooking a key component of a treatment plan can undermine positive outcomes.

In this chapter, interventions developed for specific behavioral sleep disorders are described. Additionally strategies for establishing healthy sleep hygiene and bedtime routines will be described. The treatment of co-occurring mental health conditions that contribute to sleep problems and the utilization of medication in the treatment of sleep disorders are discussed briefly.

Fundamentals of Sleep Intervention

The first step in developing an effective sleep intervention protocol is making sure you understand what the goal is. That is, knowing what you are working to help the child or adolescent accomplish along with knowing what the parents want. The most common goals I encounter in clinic include:

- Eliminate bedtime resistance
- Establish independent sleep onset skills
- Decrease sleep onset latency
- Eliminate night wakings
- Increase total sleep time (TST)
- Obtain sleep at night
- Eliminate parasomnia episodes

While these goals may be pursued independently, they tend to co-occur. Oftentimes when working to increase TST, eliminating night wakings and decreasing sleep onset latency are the keys to achieving increased TST. Additionally, establishing independent sleep onset skills often co-occurs with eliminating bedtime resistance and decreasing sleep onset latency. Two goals that are nearly always pursued jointly are establishing independent sleep onset skills and eliminating night wakings. You might recall from Chapter 2 that falling asleep is a learned behavior and night wakings occur throughout the night as part of the natural sleep–wake cycle. When a child needs parental presence or some other specific condition to fall asleep at bedtime, the same conditions are often required to resume sleeping following naturally occurring night wakings. When the conditions are absent during a night waking, the child experiences difficulty falling back to sleep and most often requires parental assistance in reestablishing the necessary conditions for sleep onset. This set of circumstances results in disrupted sleep for the child and the parents.

Parents typically have one or more specific goals in mind when they pursue clinical services for sleep problems. As their goals are defined and the assessment is conducted, it is common for additional goals to be identified. For example, when eliminating parasomnias is the parent's goal, an additional goal becomes increasing TST. In this circumstance, increasing TST is the first goal pursued and an important and necessary component of the sleep intervention protocol. When children and adolescents present to the clinic with concerns related to sleep schedule, the parents are focused on establishing a preferred schedule as the treatment goal. Oftentimes goals related to sleep hygiene, sleep onset latency, and independent sleep onset skills are also established. Again the goals frequently overlap with the components of the sleep intervention protocol.

There are goals that are important from a clinical perspective that parents, children, and adolescents typically have not considered. The most common one is establishing healthy sleep hygiene. Children, adolescents, and their parents generally lack awareness of what sleep hygiene encompasses and how important healthy sleep hygiene is to healthy sleep. While parents do present to clinic knowing they want to increase the TST for their child or teen, it is often the case that the child or teen is sleep deprived and he or she and their parents are unaware of this fact. Thus, increasing

TST is a goal often promoted by the clinician. Two additional goals typically identified by the clinician are to eliminate snoring and improve sleep quality. The detrimental effects of snoring and sleep-related breathing disorders are becoming increasingly substantiated (Sulit et al. 2005). Thus, it is important to assess for and treat snoring and other sleep-related breathing problems to improve sleep quality. Sleep quality is also impacted by frequent night wakings and parasomnias. While parents may present with the goal to eliminate night wakings, they do not often consider sleep quality as an important outcome. Working to understand the goals for pursuing services for sleep problems and facilitating recognition of additional important goals is the foundation to establishing an effective sleep intervention protocol and increases the likelihood of adherence to the protocol.

Psychoeducation is a central component to developing an effective sleep intervention protocol. Children, teens, and parents are often unaware of important facts related to sleep. Starting with education around the concept that falling asleep is a learned behavior is often practical. Helping parents, older children, and teens recognize how they have learned to fall asleep and how that learning history interferes with treatment goals is crucial. Helping them further to understand and accept the importance of healthy sleep hygiene, most specifically nothing but sleep in bed, and healthy bedtime routines as critical to the process of learning that the bed and bedtime signal sleep versus staying awake. As the assessment is conducted, all of the barriers to achieving a paired association between the bed and going to sleep are identified. These barriers are then systematically addressed in the sleep intervention protocol. As you are working with the parents, children, and teens, you are providing information about how to create conditions that will promote sleep during the desired hours.

Another important psychoeducation point is the fact that one cannot make someone else sleep. We can, however, increase the likelihood that someone will fall asleep. This is one of the very important ways the sleep diary is critical to developing an effective sleep intervention protocol. The sleep diary tells us when the child or teen has been falling asleep, allowing us to predict what time the child or teen will most likely fall asleep. Communicating to parents, older children, and teens that controlling when they sleep and when they are awake is important to achieving sleep-related goals. This most often translates into ensuring a consistent morning wake time everyday and eliminating napping for children ages 5 years and older. These two recommendations often result in complaints from teens and older children, so helping them understand the significance of these recommendations is important.

Finally, psychoeducation about the recommended TST for the child or adolescent is always necessary. Parents, children, and teens do not know how much sleep is recommended the vast majority of the time. And they are often surprised by how many hours of sleep are recommended for someone their age. When this information is discussed, I often calculate how much sleep the child or teen is currently achieving. I then calculate the nightly sleep deficit based on the recommended TST and multiply this number by five or seven depending on how much weekday and weekend sleep schedules vary. This allows me to share with children, teens and parents the sleep deficit acquired in a week. It is not uncommon for a child or teen to lose a full night's sleep each week. This realization may help increase motivation to work to increase TST nightly.

For parents of children who are of napping age, psychoeducation regarding recommended TST also involves informing them about how much sleep to expect overnight and how much to expect during naps. It is my clinical experience that parents of very young children overestimate how much sleep their child should get overnight. This overestimation results in unrealistic expectations about what time the child should fall asleep and what time the child should wake up. These expectations then lead to the child being in bed too long overnight.

In sharing information about recommended TSTs and realistic expectations for overnight sleep, I work with parents, children, and teens to identify the hours they would prefer the child to sleep. In practice, this typically involves working backward from the required morning wake time to establish bedtime based on the number of hours of sleep to be achieved. When this process results in an unrealistic bedtime, really early for a teenager for example, we reevaluate the morning wake time. This usually involves discussing the morning routine and looking for ways to delay morning wake time by 15 to 30 minutes or more. It is somewhat surprising how often this recommendation is met with resistance. Taking the time to understand the rationales and motivations of the child, teen, and parents facilitates generating doable and acceptable recommendations.

The sleep intervention protocol developed must also address the function of the sleep problem in order to be effective. Functions vary for sleep problems and by the child or teen presenting with the sleep disorder. For example, children who present with a sleep onset association disorder who are rocked to sleep, the problem of being rocked to sleep serves the function of achieving sleep onset. Thus, the sleep intervention protocol must address achieving sleep onset without rocking. Similarly for children who present with a rhythmic movement disorder, the movement functions to facilitate sleep onset. In developing an intervention protocol for these children, establishing a new way of falling asleep, one that includes lying still, is necessary. Habit reversal is useful model when treating rhythmic movement disorder.

When children are able to access milk, juice, or other preferred foods or activities during night wakings, their night wakings serve the function of accessing preferred activities. Eliminating this access and addressing the procedures for doing so in the sleep intervention protocol are important. Teens who present with delayed sleep phase and miss school most mornings may want to avoid school. Thus, the delayed sleep phase serves the function of school avoidance, and the sleep intervention protocol must address this function. Children and teens who present with worries or fears at bedtime may avoid going to bed and/or falling asleep resulting in extended sleep onset latency. When children want to talk about their fears at bedtime, this behavior often serves the function of bedtime avoidance. Discussing worries or fears at bedtime must be addressed in developing an effective sleep intervention protocol. As functions are identified, explaining the function of the behavior and how to address it are important conversations as you develop sleep intervention protocols with the parents, children, and adolescents.

Another objective of an effective sleep intervention protocol is to address the barriers to achieving the sleep-related treatment goals. At times, the barriers overlap with the functions of the sleep problem. However, this is not always the case. In the case of the teen whose sleep phase delay serves to allow the teen to avoid school, wanting to avoid school may be a barrier to following a sleep intervention protocol. Thus, addressing the reasons for school avoidance will likely be necessary, or at the very least, increasing motivation to attend school. Issues that interfere with sleep that are unrelated to the child's or teen's behavior have more to do with the environment. Ensuring that light exposure is addressed, finding alternative locations and times for activities historically conducted in the bed, and establishing a transition object are a few examples. Basically, whatever is identified as interfering with achieving the treatment goals must be addressed. Being informed about what may potentially interfere with sleep and assessing for these factors are the clinician's responsibility.

At times, it may be helpful to include a motivational or incentive program as a component of the sleep intervention protocol. Learning new skills and changing behavior can be challenging. Increasing motivation to engage in the required effort by establishing a meaningful incentive can be helpful. Children are often eager to earn small prizes or preferred breakfast items by falling asleep alone and remaining in bed all night. Teens and older children can be motivated to follow sleep schedules by contingent access to available privileges or preferred privileges. The decision to include a motivational or incentive program is discussed with the parents and the child or teen. When the decision to include this component in the protocol is made, establishing the incentive with the child or teen (with parent agreement) is critical to effectiveness.

The sleep intervention protocol must be comprehensive to be optimally effective. It has been my clinical experience that parents frequently have tried some or most of the strategies included in the sleep intervention protocols we establish. The primary difference is their efforts typically consisted of trying one strategy and then trying another without managing all of the components necessary to produce the desired outcome. Remember, you cannot force someone to sleep. You can create the likelihood that the child or adolescent will sleep at the preferred time. To do this, the sleep intervention protocol must address bedtime, morning wake time, and napping. To increase the likelihood that a child or teen will sleep when they go to bed, we must control when they go to bed, when they get up and limit or prohibit napping. When children and teens are allowed to make up sleep by sleeping in or napping, we will not be successful in shifting their sleep onset time at bedtime. Managing the sleep–wake schedule along with the factors addressed above is key to developing an effective sleep intervention protocol.

The final step in developing an effective sleep intervention protocol is to carefully determine what the child, adolescent, and parents are willing to do and what they are unwilling to do. There are several specific protocols that are effective interventions for specific sleep disorders. The social acceptability of these protocols varies widely. Recommending an approach that the child, adolescent, or parent will not implement is pointless and may prove detrimental to the clinical relationship as well as clinical outcomes. Working with children, teens, and parents to identify effective strategies they are willing to implement is key to achieving the identified sleep-related treatment goals.

Specific Protocols

A foundational step in establishing a specific sleep protocol for a child or adolescent is to address sleep hygiene. There are basic aspects of sleep hygiene that are key to establishing healthy sleep habits. Discussing a regular sleep–wake schedule that can be adhered to day-to-day and allows for sufficient TST is a helpful topic to address first. Then discussing the bedroom environment and establishing steps to be taken to ensure the child or adolescent is falling asleep in a quiet dark room are needed. Keep in mind a standard night light and white noise are acceptable. More light than that needs to be eliminated either gradually by reducing the number of lights left on and/or reducing the wattage in the bulbs every couple of nights to reduce the light available. Ensuring the bedtime routine is completed just before bedtime is also important to ensure daytime activities end once the bedtime routine is initiated. Establishing the rule of nothing but sleep in bed and problem-solving barriers to following this rule are also important to the success of the child or adolescent in adhering to the sleep protocol. For young children who are accustomed to parental presence at bedtime, it is helpful to discuss the existence of a transition object like a special blanket or stuffed animal. If the child does not have a transition object, establishing one is conducive to establishing independent sleep onset skills. Finally, discussing the child or adolescent's typical schedule to ensure caffeine is not consumed after 7 p.m., exercise is completed at least 2 hours prior to bedtime and limiting electronic use due to the exposure to the light emitted by the screens at least an hour before bedtime is recommended.

Sleep Restriction

Sleep restriction is the practice of limiting TST to an amount less than the recommended TST temporarily and systematically. Sleep restriction is particularly useful in addressing excessive sleep onset latencies associated with sleep onset association problems, insomnia and insomnia associated with bedtime resistance and worry or rumination. The sleep diary is crucial to incorporating sleep restriction in the sleep intervention protocol. The sleep diary reveals the typical time of sleep onset. The practice of sleep restriction requires the bedtime to be set at or just past the current sleep onset time. In practice, I typically show the parents the sleep diary and invite them to identify the time we can be most confident the child or teen will fall asleep each night. They tend to recognize the most predictable time and when they do not I help them see the time that is most predictable. We also discuss the sleep–wake schedule they ultimately want to achieve.

The other key components of sleep restriction are controlling the morning wake time and any napping. Again the premise is to restrict the TST initially to achieve ready sleep onset once the child or adolescent is in bed. TST is increased gradually in response to ready sleep onset. Ready sleep onset is defined as the child or teen falls asleep within 20 minutes of bedtime on three consecutive nights. When this pattern is established, the bedtime is moved 15 minutes earlier. Ready sleep onset is again monitored and when achieved on three consecutive nights the bedtime is again moved 15 minutes earlier. This process is repeated until the predetermined preferred bedtime is achieved.

When sleep restriction is first introduced, the parents tend to have a reluctant response while older children and teens are delighted. Explaining that the recommended initial bedtime is temporary helps assuage their concerns. It is also helpful to explain that the child or teen is not asleep before the recommended initial bedtime as it is. When the current struggles include bedtime resistance or sleep onset association problems, parents become increasingly receptive to sleep restriction as they understand the positive impact potential for establishing a strong paired association between the bed and sleep for the child.

In my clinical practice, I rarely establish a sleep intervention protocol that does not include sleep restriction. This is attributable to the sleep concerns that present in my clinical practice. Similar to sleep restriction is restricting total time in bed. When a child presents with frequent or extended night wakings, ready sleep onset and sufficient TST and the absence of breathing-related difficulties, then time in bed is restricted. You may recall that excessive time in bed may result in extended night wakings for children. The schedule is typically adjusted by moving either the bedtime or morning wake time to encompass the total number of hours of recommended TST. This protocol serves to consolidate sleep while maintaining the TST being achieved. These adjustments are made in collaboration with the parents to ensure that the sleep–wake schedule fits their lifestyle and needs.

Bedtime Pass

The Bedtime Pass is a card or other object that is good for one call out or opportunity to come out of the bedroom after bedtime. I recommend using a card, as it is easy to place under the pillow and does not serve another function for the child as a stuffed animal or other object might. The child is encouraged to help make the Bedtime Pass (or select and order one online at www.thebedtimepass.com). I typically explain the rules of the Bedtime Pass in clinic and share instructions with the parents to review with the child. An available tool for introducing and implementing the Bedtime Pass is the children's storybook by the same name (Schnoes 2017). The storybook includes parental instructions and helps parents and clinicians teach children about how the Bedtime Pass works and how to implement it effectively in a fun accessible format.

At bedtime, the child is instructed to keep the Bedtime Pass under his or her pillow. When the child calls out or comes out of the bedroom a parent immediately responds to the child's request or need. This does not mean the request is granted, it may be denied. Either way the parent then collects the Bedtime Pass and returns the child to bed if he or she came out of the bedroom. Once the Bedtime Pass is collected, any and all subsequent attempts to call out from the bedroom by the child are ignored. If the child comes out of the bedroom once the Bedtime Pass has been used, he or she is returned to bed without any verbal interaction or acknowledgment of further requests. The effectiveness of the Bedtime Pass in eliminating bedtime resistance without an extinction burst has been demonstrated in several studies (Freeman 2006; Friman et al. 1999; Moore et al. 2007). For a more complete description of the Bedtime Pass, see Schnoes (2011).

Sleep Fairy

The Sleep Fairy is a social story that teaches children about desired bedtime behavior. The story incorporates the identity of a Sleep Fairy that keeps watch for children who exhibit desired bedtime behavior and delivers contingent positive reinforcement. In practice, the parents deliver positive reinforcement in the form of a prize or token under the child's pillow or bed once the child has fallen asleep, when the child exhibited the desired bedtime behavior. The storybook by the same name includes parental instructions that address implementation and a fading procedure for the intervention (Peterson and Peterson 2003). One study has been published demonstrating the effectiveness of the intervention and its social acceptability (Burke, Kuhn, and Peterson 2004).

Cry it Out

The cry-it-out procedure is as it sounds. A parent places the child in bed (or the crib), tells the child good night, turns off the lights, leaves the room, and ignores all crying. This procedure may also include closing the door, a decision that is made with the parents. When the child wakes in the night the same procedures are followed. If the child comes out of his or her bedroom he or she is returned to the bed without any attention or interaction other than physical guidance back to bed. Highly effective, this procedure lacks parent acceptability (Kuhn and Elliott 2003). Children tend to exhibit an extinction burst. That is they cry for an extended period of time the first night, with a shorter duration the second night, and further reduction the third night. In just a few nights, ready sleep onset is typically achieved. Parents struggle to tolerate the crying and distress exhibited by their children and in my clinical practice rarely agree to this protocol.

Quick Check

The quick check procedure is a variation on the cry-it-out procedure. The quick check method incorporates having the parent intermittently check on the child to ensure he or she is safe and well. In implementing this procedure, the clinician determines in advance with the parents how long they will be able to ignore the child's crying before needing to check on the child. This may be a minute or two or up to 15 to 20 minutes or more. The interval does not matter; what matters is the parent's ability to adhere to the interval. It is important to establish an interval they can successfully adhere to rather than one that is too long. If the interval is too long, the parents will likely experience elevated distress and struggle to follow the procedure with integrity.

At bedtime, the parent puts the child to bed, tells the child good night, turns off the lights, closes the door (optional), leaves the room, and ignores all crying until predetermined interval of time (e.g., 5 min) elapses. The parent then goes into the child's room and silently and quickly (30 seconds or less) checks on the child. The parent does not pick the child up, offer nurturing touch or speak to the child. The parent may return a fallen blanket or pacifier without speaking to the child. The parent repeats the procedure each time the predetermined interval of time elapses until the child falls asleep. The same procedure is followed for night-time awakenings.

Quick check is an effective intervention with somewhat more parent acceptability than the cry-it-out method (Kuhn and Elliott 2003). This procedure typically results in extended crying the first night or two with gradual reduction night-to-night. When implemented with integrity, it results in ready independent sleep onset. The extinction burst exhibited by children makes this procedure less attractive and tolerable for parents.

Graduated Extinction

The graduated extinction procedure is a variation on the quick check method. Similar to the quick check method, the clinician determines with the parents how long they will ignore the child's crying. The interval of time that parents ignore the child's crying is then gradually increased between each check. The increase in intervals is also determined with the parents. In practice, they might look like waiting 5 minutes before checking the first time, then waiting 10 minutes, then 15 minutes, then 20 minutes, and so on until the child falls asleep. At bedtime, the parent puts the child to bed, tells the child good night, turns off the lights, leaves the room, and closes the door (optional). The parent then ignores all crying until the predetermined time interval elapses. The parent then silently and quickly (less than 30 seconds) checks on the child. The parent does not touch, pick up, or talk to the child. The parent may return a dropped blanket or pacifier without speaking to the child. Each subsequent check occurs according to the predetermined schedule with each interval between checks increasing as planned until the child falls asleep. The same procedure is followed for nighttime wakings. This procedure serves to alleviate the parent's concern that something might be "wrong" with the child while simultaneously allowing the child increased time to achieve sleep onset between checks.

The graduate extinction method is an effective intervention with somewhat more parent acceptability than the cry-it-out method (Kuhn and Elliott 2003). Like the cry-it-out and quick check methods, this procedure typically results in extended crying the first night or two with gradual reduction night-to-night. When implemented with integrity, it results in ready independent sleep onset. The extinction burst exhibited by children makes this procedure also less attractive and tolerable for parents.

Delayed Bedtime

The delayed bedtime procedure involves putting the child to bed at a time when the parents are confident the child will be too tired to resist falling asleep. This procedure typically involves noting the time the child usually falls asleep and delaying bedtime for 30 to 60 minutes. Once the child is placed in bed, the parents ignore the child's crying, calling out and any efforts to engage the parents for 15 to 30 minutes. If the child comes out of the bedroom, he or she is returned to bed without any verbal interaction with the parent. If the child is still awake once the predetermined interval of time to ignore the child elapses, the child is removed from bed and kept up and awake for 1 hour. The child is then returned to bed an hour later and ignored for the 15 to 30 minutes a second time. This procedure is repeated until the child falls asleep. Once the child reliably goes to bed and falls asleep at the later bedtime, the bedtime is gradually moved earlier.

Co-Sleeping

Co-sleeping, or allowing the child to sleep with his or her parents or a sibling, is another viable sleep intervention. Co-sleeping eliminates the expectation that the child will sleep alone. When co-sleeping is the choice, the child is allowed to sleep with the parent or a sibling all night every night. The child may sleep with the parent or sibling in the parent or sibling's bed or in the child's bed.

In my clinical experience, parents are often embarrassed to admit they engage in co-sleeping and that they prefer co-sleeping. There is nothing wrong with co-sleeping. I often encourage and support parents in deciding where and how they want their child to sleep. I also provide psychoeducation regarding the cultural impact of Western society on the perception of co-sleeping as "wrong" or "bad." Many cultures in the world engage in co-sleeping. It is a viable option for children and families. I also inform parents who choose co-sleeping as their preference that when they are ready for the child to sleep independently, the child will need to learn how to do so and professional assistance in facilitating this learning process may be useful.

Parental Presence

Parental presence involves having the parent present in the child's bedroom until the child falls asleep. The parent may fall asleep in the child's bedroom, waking later to sleep in his or her own bed. The parental presence procedure is strictly about presence. That is the parent is in the child's bedroom and lies on the floor or in a separate bed. The parent does not lie with the child in his or her bed. The parent is also communicating it is time to go to sleep by completely ignoring the child and modeling sleep compatible behavior (e.g., being quiet, lying still, eyes closed). Once the bedtime routine is completed and the parent has told the child good night, all talking ceases. Any attempts by the child to engage the parent are ignored. Once the child falls asleep, the parent leaves the child's bedroom. The parent must repeat the same procedures for night awakenings.

Children may have a difficult time accepting the parent's presence and inability to interact with the parent. When this happens, the child persists in talking to or gaining the parent's attention. Parents must send a consistent message that it is bedtime and resist all attempts by the child to interact. This may be difficult for parents, as the child will likely demonstrate an extinction burst, that is, increased effort in terms of intensity, severity, and duration to gain the parent's attention. The other limitation of this procedure is the need to implement it for night awakenings resulting in sleep disruption for the parents and the child.

Excuse-Me Drill

The excuse-me drill is a variation on parental presence at bedtime. It is a strategy that ultimately teaches the child to fall asleep independently. This method involves having the parent remain in the bedroom with the child at bedtime. The parent sits on a chair next to the child's bed or on the floor. The parent does not lie in bed with the child or sit next to the child in bed. The parent may briefly praise sleep compatible behaviors (lying still, eyes closed, quiet, and so on), intermittently pairing brief touch (e.g., stroke his or her back,) with the praise. When the child is nearly falling asleep, the drill involves the parent saying something like "Excuse me, I need to check on something. I'll be right back." Initially the parent steps away from the child and returns to the child's bedroom before the child falls asleep. By returning before the child falls asleep, the child learns the parent does in fact return. The very first time the parent may only get to the child's door, not even leaving the child's bedroom, in order to return before the child is able to call out or come out of the bedroom. The procedure is repeated nightly very gradually increasing the duration of time the parent is away from the child. Upon returning, the parent praises sleep compatible behavior. If the child becomes disruptive while the parent is out of the bedroom, the parent is instructed to remain out of the bedroom and ignore the disruptive behavior and return only after the child quiets again. Eventually the child will fall asleep while the parent is out of the bedroom. The same procedure is repeated for night awakenings. Ultimately the parent will be able to put the child to bed say good night, let the child know the parent will be back to check on the child and walk out of the room. The child will be able to fall asleep independently. Once this is achieved, I recommend parents periodically check on the child before he or she falls asleep to reinforce sleep compatible behaviors.

In my clinical practice, the excuse-me drill is acceptable to parents and effective. I suspect its acceptability is related to the limited distress exhibited by the child at bedtime. Limitations include the more delayed process for achieving independent sleep onset and the need to repeat the bedtime procedure for night waking until the child learns to fall asleep independently. For a more complete description of the excuse-me drill, see Kuhn (2011).

Scheduled Awakening

Scheduled awakening is a procedure that involves waking a child before the anticipated sleep disruption occurs. This procedure can be used for partial arousal parasomnias such as night terrors and sleep walking. Scheduled awakening can also be used to address nighttime bedwetting. Although nighttime bedwetting is not a sleep disorder, it can and often does interrupt the sleep of children and teens. It is important to note that nighttime bedwetting is not treated in children under the age of 5 years.

Parents begin by keeping track of the time each night the child experiences an awakening. The parent then wakes the child 15 to 30 minutes prior to the recorded time of awakenings. The parent then engages the child in the typical bedtime routine at the point of tucking the child in to bed. The parent then increases the time between scheduled awakenings on subsequent nights. When there is only one scheduled awakening early in the sleep cycle, the time between the scheduled awakening and the spontaneous awakening is increased. That is, the parent wakes the child 30 minutes, then 40 minutes before the expected spontaneous awakening. When the spontaneous awakening disappears and the scheduled awakenings are more than 45 minutes prior to the expected spontaneous awakening, the scheduled awakenings are stopped.

When using this procedure for nighttime bedwetting, the parent wakes the child prior to the anticipated night-wetting episode. Night-wetting episodes can be established in a couple of ways. Parents may check the child hourly or every 30 minutes for a few nights and document when the child is wet or dry. When the parent detects the child is wet, the child is awakened and put in dry clothes. This procedure is recommended when parents and children or teens are unaware of the time of the night-wetting episode. Some children spontaneously wake when they wet at night. In this instance, parents can document the time of the awakening over the course of a few nights. With information regarding the timing of night-wetting episodes in hand, the scheduled awakening is established 15 to 20 minutes before the anticipated night-wetting episode. Upon awakening, the child or teen, the parent takes or sends the child to the bathroom to urinate. The time of the scheduled awakening is delayed on subsequent nights in 12- to 20-minute increments as long as the child is dry when the scheduled awakening occurs. This procedure is repeated until the child is awakened according to the usual morning schedule and is dry.

Chronotherapy

Chronotherapy is a protocol that is typically used to address sleep phase delay exhibited by adolescents. It works with the adolescent's current sleep schedule to establish a new sleep–wake schedule on a daily basis until the preferred sleep–wake schedule is established. Chronotherapy allows for 8 hours of sleep every 27 hours with no napping allowed. The adolescent engages in his or her bedtime routine at the scheduled sleep onset time. This procedure also encourages routine waking behavior during the nonsleeping hours. The initial bedtime is established based on the adolescent's current sleep onset schedule. Once the current sleep schedule is clear, the bedtime is delayed 3 hours from 1 day to the next. The adolescent goes to bed as scheduled, wakes after 8 hours of sleep, and remains awake until 3 hours past the previous day's bedtime. For an adolescent who falls asleep routinely at 3 a.m., chronotherapy would result in bedtimes of 6 a.m., 9 a.m., 12 p.m., and so on until the preferred bedtime is established. On this schedule, the adolescent will be awake for 19 hours, sleep for 8 hours, awake for 19 hours repeating this sleep–wake cycle until the preferred bedtime is reached.

Table 4.1 summarizes the key components of sleep protocols based on the presenting sleep problems. It is meant to serve as a guide to ensure that the necessary components are addressed and the protocols most likely to be effective are considered. The comprehensive assessment provides critical information for the development of the sleep intervention protocol and decision making regarding specific protocols to implement. The term motivation deficit refers to children and adolescents who consistently fall asleep alone in a quiet dark room. They may exhibit excessive sleep onset latency and they ultimately fall asleep alone. They have the skills to fall asleep alone and lack the motivation to do so readily. Skill deficit refers to those children and adolescents who do not fall asleep independently. They require parental presence or the presence of other stimuli (music, light, television, and so on) to fall asleep. For these children and adolescents, they lack the skills necessary to readily fall asleep alone.

In my clinical practice, specific protocols are typically combined simultaneously and/or sequentially. I always address sleep hygiene and very often employ sleep restriction and an additional specific protocol for sleep problems related to excessive sleep onset latency. For children and adolescents who exhibit skill deficits or problematic sleep onset

Table 4.1 *Potential protocols for specific sleep problems*

Motivation Deficit	Skill Deficit
• Sleep Hygiene	• Sleep Hygiene
• Sleep Restriction	• Sleep Restriction
• Motivation or Incentive Program	• Motivation or Incentive Program
• Bedtime Pass OR	• Parental Presence OR
• Sleep Fairy	• Excuse Me Drill OR
Insomnia	• Cry It Out OR
• Sleep Hygiene	• Quick Check OR
• Sleep Restriction	• Graduated extinction
• Cognitive Behavior Therapy (CBT) Strategies	
Sleep Phase Delay	**Parasomnias**
• Sleep Hygiene	• Increase TST OR
• Motivation or Incentive Program	• Improve Quality OR
• Chronotherapy OR	• Scheduled Awakening
• Sleep Restriction	

associations, multiple protocols are typically implemented sequentially. Again, sleep hygiene and sleep restriction are employed simultaneously and often in combination with the specific protocol for parental presence. Once ready sleep onset is established in the child or adolescent's bed in a quiet dark room with parental presence, the protocol shifts and the excuse-me drill replaces parental presence. Once independent sleep onset is established, the sleep restriction is gradually decreased. For children who have learned to fall asleep in their parents' bed, parental presence is employed to facilitate the child learning to fall asleep in his or her own bed with the parent lying next to him or her, then sitting next to him or her and then sitting in the room next to the bed. Remember falling asleep is a learned behavior. To facilitate learning to fall asleep independently, making fewer changes at one time increases the child's ability to fall asleep more readily with less disruption and/or distress. This gradual process may take longer. In my clinical experience, the excuse-me drill is often preferred by parents.

Special Circumstances

This section addresses how to manage intervention and treatment for concerns specific to obstructive sleep apnea (OSA), narcolepsy, and comorbid mood disorders. Sleep apnea and narcolepsy require medical involvement in the diagnosis and treatment of these disorders. When mood disorders co-occur with insomnia, it is important to address the mood disorder as well as the insomnia. Clinicians work with children, teens, and parents in determining treatment priorities and the course of treatment. When OSA or narcolepsy is suspected, further assessment is a priority. When comorbid mood disorders are present, clinical impressions guide treatment priority recommendations.

Sleep Apnea

The first step in treating suspected sleep apnea is working with the child's or adolescent's primary medical care provider to share your clinical impressions and recommendations. The next step may result in a referral for an overnight sleep study or polysomnography (PSG) or referral to an ear, nose, and throat (ENT) specialist. When children present with snoring and daytime concerns exacerbated by insufficient TST or impaired sleep quality, consultation with an ENT is helpful to determine if the tonsil or adenoids may be causing airway obstruction during sleep. When airway obstruction is a concern, a common first line intervention is a tonsillectomy and/or adenoidectomy. Another option is referral for an overnight PSG to determine if the child experiences apnea during sleep. When children and adolescents exhibit difficulty breathing while sleeping that results in depleted blood oxygen levels and meets criteria for sleep apnea, treatment is necessary. Treatment may include a tonsillectomy and/or adenoidectomy and/or prescription for a continuous positive airway pressure (CPAP) device. Another treatment option is an oral appliance that serves to keep the airway open during sleep.

A CPAP device provides a continuous flow of oxygen into the airway through the nose and/or mouth. Some CPAPs have a mask that fits over the nose and mouth while others employ nasal cannulas to deliver the oxygen. CPAPs also typically include a humidifier to prevent dry airways during sleep.

Although CPAPs are highly effective, treatment adherence is poor. Wearing a CPAP can be uncomfortable and interferes with treatment compliance. Several sources of discomfort exist including: fit of the mask, movement limits while wearing the mask, the noise of the CPAP machine, airway dryness, air flow pressure that is too high or too low. Treatment compliance can be improved when a gradual well-monitored process is implemented. The first step is to work with the child or adolescent closely to ensure air flow pressure is comfortable and effective as well as adequate humidification of the air to prevent airway dryness. The next step is begin with wearing the CPAP for an hour or two at night and gradually increasing the amount of time the CPAP is worn over time. Getting accustomed to wearing a CPAP takes time and represents a new condition that must be incorporated into learning how to fall asleep. Pairing sleep restriction with the initiation of CPAP can facilitate this learning process. The benefits of improved sleep quality have strong reinforcement value when the child or adolescent is able to wear a CPAP comfortably long enough to experience the benefits.

Narcolepsy

As discussed in previous chapters, narcolepsy requires PSG and multiple sleep latency test for diagnosis. Narcolepsy is considered a medical condition, and first line treatment is medication.

When narcolepsy is suspected, coordination and consultation with the child's primary care provider is critical to obtaining referral for the appropriate sleep studies and effective treatment.

Comorbid Mood Disorders

When children and adolescents present with sleep and mood disorders, it is important to address both concerns. Cognitive and behavioral strategies are often effective in treating mood disorders. In my clinical practice, worries, rumination and/or obsessions and compulsions interfere with sleep onset. Addressing these concerns directly and independently will likely be necessary. When such concerns co-occur with sleep onset difficulties, it is recommended to treat the anxiety-related symptoms before addressing the sleep onset association. Clinicians are encouraged to focus treatment on daytime symptoms initially, as children and adolescents will likely experience more success and this momentum can facilitate treatment that targets nighttime or bedtime symptoms.

When children and adolescents present with depression and sleep disturbance, it is again important to address both concerns. It may be that clinical concerns are addressed simultaneously or sequentially. Behavioral activation is an efficacious treatment for depression. Including behavioral activation in the treatment plan may not only improve mood, but it may also serve to limit excessive sleeping and promote sleep onset according to a preferred schedule. Similarly, limiting time in bed and time in the bedroom may facilitate improvements in mood. Cognitive behavior therapy is another viable intervention that facilitates understanding of mood and how it relates to thoughts and behavior including sleep behavior. Cognitive behavior therapy for insomnia may facilitate helping older children and teens understand the importance of sleep and healthy sleep habits with specific implications for mood. Regardless of the order, addressing both concerns is important. The clinical priority and course of treatment are established with the child or teen and his or her parents.

Medication

A number of medications are prescribed to treat sleep-related concerns in children and adolescents. One of the more common medications prescribed for children is melatonin. Melatonin is the hormone the body naturally produces to facilitate sleep onset. Although it is often thought of as a sedative, melatonin's mechanism of action is to advance the sleep–wake cycle. Recent research has revealed very small doses of melatonin given a few hours before bedtime may be effective in facilitating sleep onset (Kennaway 2015). In addition to melatonin, there are a number prescription and over the counter medications utilized in treating sleep problems in children and adolescents. Medications are most often prescribed when children struggle to fall asleep readily and/or struggle to maintain sleep. A common challenge in the utilization of medication for sleep problems is the temporary benefit experienced by the child or adolescent. The medication may work for a period of time and then lose its effectiveness. Or the medication may facilitate sleep onset and result in limited if any benefit for night wakings. When medications are effective, it is not uncommon for the initial gains to diminish when the medication is withdrawn (Mindell et al. 2006).

There are sleep disorders that require medication as part of the treatment protocol. Such disorders include narcolepsy, restless leg syndrome, and periodic leg movement disorders. A thorough discussion of medications utilized for sleep is beyond the scope of this book. Readers are encouraged to review articles exploring the utilization of medication among children and adolescents (Schnoes et al. 2006; Owens, Rosen, and Mindell 2003; Rosen, Owens, and Mindell 2005).

It is important for clinicians to seek consent to collaborate with prescribing physicians for children and adolescents they treat who are being prescribed psychotropic medications. Whether medications are prescribed specifically for sleep or another mental health or medical concern, understanding the implications of the medication for the child's or adolescent's sleep is imperative. In my clinical practice, it is not uncommon for children to present to clinic with a behavioral sleep disorder and a history of medication treatment for the sleep problem. It is typically my goal to work with the child and his or her parents to achieve treatment goals and work to eliminate the need for continued medication management. This requires working diligently with the child and parents and coordinating care with the prescribing physician to ensure agreement with treatment goals and the course of treatment.

Conclusion

The effective treatment of sleep disorders is reliant on a detailed and comprehensive assessment of sleep habits and sleep-related behavior. To be effective and efficient, clinicians must establish with children, teens, and parents the importance if not necessity of addressing sleep concerns. Once agreement and support for treating sleep problems are established, developing a comprehensive, realistic, and clinically informed sleep intervention protocol is the next step. Oftentimes this process involves ongoing psychoeducation of children, teens, and parents to promote understanding and adherence to the recommended sleep intervention protocol. Given the current knowledge of the significant implications of impaired sleep for growth, learning, development, mood, behavior, and medical health, to neglect addressing sleep-related concerns directly or via referral to a sleep specialist would be clinically irresponsible.

CHAPTER 5

Case Studies

Several case studies are provided in this chapter to illustrate the assessment, sleep intervention protocol development, treatment and treatment follow up for behavioral pediatric sleep concerns. Case studies are included for the following clinical presentations: behavioral insomnia of childhood: limit-setting type and sleep onset association type, insomnia, and comorbid anxiety. Two of the case examples involve young children whereas two examples include a teen and a preteen. The names of the children have been changed. The anxiety case example is comorbid with the sleep onset association type rather than just insomnia. The demographic information and descriptions of the clinical presentations remain intact.

Behavioral Insomnia of Childhood: Limit-Setting Type

Danny was a 2-year-old Caucasian male who presented to clinic for bedtime resistance and frequent night wakings. He lived with his parents and infant sibling. His medical history was remarkable for milk soy protein intolerance. His psychiatric history was unremarkable.

Danny's parents described longstanding difficulties with sleep for Danny. They reported that since infancy, he was a very fussy baby, and historically the only way they could get him to sleep at night was to put him in the car and drive him around. At the time of the intake Danny reportedly resisted bedtime for nearly 90 minutes nightly. His parents reported he would finally fall asleep on his own either on the floor or on the mattress in his room. His parents reported that he woke approximately one time per night every 10 days. Danny's mother described lying down with Danny in his room when he woke in the night. She added that previously, Danny woke multiple times every night and at most slept 4 to 5 hours at a time. Danny did not sleep through the night until he was 2 years and 2 weeks old. Danny's parents reported he woke on his own at 7:30 a.m. daily. Danny's mother reported that she continued to drive him around to get him to fall asleep for a nap, before bringing him home and moving him to his bed. Danny napped for 1.5 to 2 hours every day between 2 and 5 p.m. and had to be awakened daily from his nap. Danny's parents reported wanting Danny to sleep between 9 p.m. and 7 a.m. nightly with a 90-minute nap. Danny's parents reported significant disruptive daytime behavior including frequent, aggressive tantrums, aggressive play, noncompliance and disruptive behavior at mealtime.

A sleep diary was completed for the eight nights prior to Danny's intake appointment. The sleep diary revealed a fairly consistent bedtime of 9:30 p.m. with delayed sleep onset ranging from 10 p.m. to 12 a.m. The most common time of sleep onset was 11 p.m. The sleep diary revealed morning awakening typically occurred at 8 a.m. with the exception of three mornings when Danny woke between 7:15 and 7:45 a.m. According to the sleep diary, Danny did not exhibit any night wakings. The sleep diary revealed Danny napped daily most often between 2 and 5 p.m. for nearly 2 hours. According to the sleep diary, Danny was achieving on average 9 hours of sleep overnight with an additional 2 hours during nap for a total of 11 hours of sleep, 30 minutes less than recommended.

The clinical interview and sleep diary record revealed significant disruptive, defiant daytime behavior and sleep-related concerns. Danny resisted bedtime for an extended period of time resulting excessive sleep onset latency at bedtime. It was my clinical impression that Danny presented with insomnia, specifically behavioral insomnia of childhood limit-setting type since he ultimately fell asleep independently on a nightly basis. This clinical impression was further supported by the absence of night waking. Driving Danny around to put him to sleep for naps seemed to reflect resistance to limits rather than a sleep onset association issue given his established independent sleep onset skills at bedtime.

Treatment focused on improving daytime behavior and establishing instruction control for five sessions prior to intervening directly on the sleep concerns. At the fifth session daytime behavior had improved with continued sleep problems. Danny's parents reported and the sleep diary revealed 2- to 3-hour sleep onset latency, frequent elopements from his room with sleep onset occurring at 11 p.m. most nights. His parents were still driving him to fall asleep for naps. Below is the sleep protocol established.

Sleep Protocol for Danny

We are working to teach Danny to sleep between 9 p.m. and 7 a.m. at night and a nap between 1 and 3 p.m. We will do this by making sure he is ready to fall asleep when he is placed in bed, ensuring his room is quiet and dark at bedtime, and moving his bedtime gradually to work with his body. To make sure that he is ready to fall asleep we will control when he goes to bed and when he wakes up. Below is the protocol we discussed.

1. Bedtime at 11 p.m.
   a. Do bedtime routine just before bedtime.
   b. Put pajamas on just before bed.
   c. Keep room quiet and dark.
2. If Danny comes to parents' bed in the night return him to his bed immediately.
3. Keep morning wake consistent at 7 a.m.
4. Move bedtime 15 minutes earlier after falling asleep 3 nights in a row within 20 minutes.
5. Repeat step 4 and hold bedtime at 9 p.m.
6. Put Danny down for a nap at 1 p.m.
   a. Put Danny in his bed for his nap.
   b. Consider a reward for staying in his bed for his nap.
   c. Do not let him sleep past 3 p.m.
7. Complete sleep diary.
8. E-mail an update in 3 days.

The first follow-up appointment for the sleep intervention protocol revealed adherence to the protocol in terms of the nighttime routine, scheduled bedtime, and morning wake time. Sleep onset latency decreased to 25 minutes and one or fewer elopements from his room. Danny's parents continued to drive him around for naps with occasional sleeping past 3 p.m. At the next appointment, sleep onset latency was reduced to 20 minutes with sleep onset at 9:45 p.m. Danny's mother

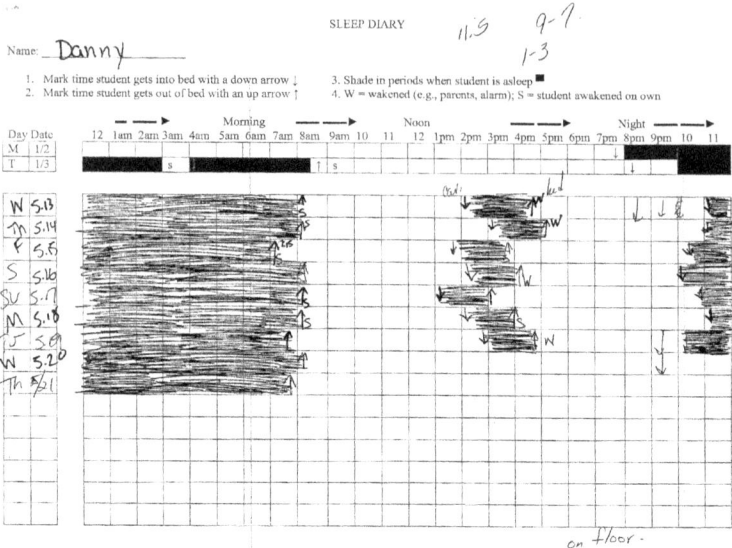

Figure 5.1 Baseline sleep diary: Danny

was transitioning Danny from the car to his bed for naps slightly awake. At the next appointment further gains were made toward achieving the 9 p.m. bedtime with ready sleep onset. A portion of the baseline and follow-up sleep diaries are presented in Figures 5.1 and 5.2.

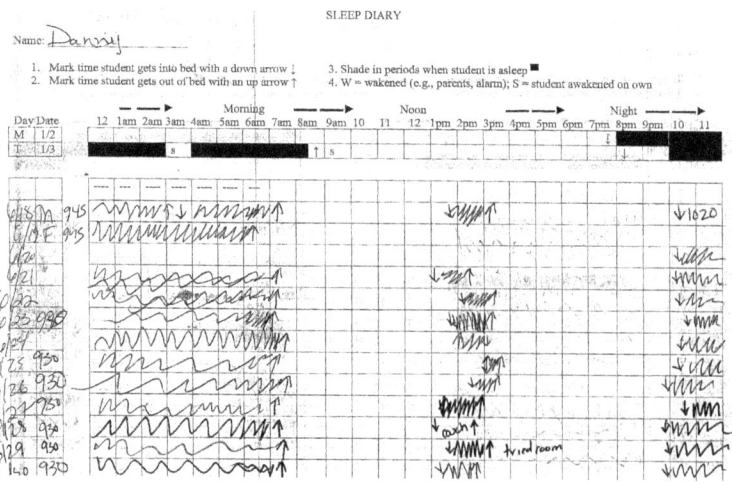

Figure 5.2 Follow-up sleep diary: Danny

Behavioral Insomnia of Childhood: Sleep Onset Association Type

Darcy was a 22-month-old Caucasian female who presented to clinic for difficulties achieving sleep onset, frequent, extended night wakings, and early morning awakening (i.e., 5 a.m.). She was the youngest of three children (siblings ages 8 years and 4 years) with married parents. Her medical and psychiatric histories were unremarkable.

Darcy's parents reported being able to get Darcy to fall asleep within 30 minutes to an hour when they rocked her to music. She woke crying within 60 to 90 minutes of falling asleep and required rocking and music to go back to sleep. She woke again at 2 or 3 a.m. and required rocking and music to return to sleep. Her parents described falling asleep while rocking Darcy for an hour or until morning. During night wakings Darcy typically requested a drink of milk. Darcy woke by 5 a.m. and was happy upon waking 60 percent of the time. Darcy's parents reported limited structure at day care with Darcy falling asleep spontaneously for naps in the living room with the television on. Darcy's parents described limited attachment to a transition object, exposure to light via bedroom windows at nap, bedtime and morning wake time. Darcy's parents described limited concerns for daytime behavior related to grazing between meals and reluctance to remain seated for meals.

A sleep diary was completed for 5 weeks preceding the intake appointment. The diary revealed a variable bedtime schedule, starting as early as 7:30 p.m. to as late as 9:30 p.m. at night. Morning wake was very consistent, the vast majority of the mornings at 5 a.m., one morning at 5:15 a.m., two mornings by 4 a.m., and three mornings at 6 a.m. The sleep diary revealed sleep onset latency ranging from 30 minutes to an hour. On two of the three most recent nights, sleep onset latency was 45 to 60 minutes. The sleep diary revealed night wakings every night, with the first night waking occurring after the first 90 minutes of sleep and lasting approximately an hour, and multiple night wakings every night in the past 5 weeks. The sleep diary also revealed napping on a daily basis, with the duration most often being an hour and occasionally 2 hours. The nap schedule was highly variable, ranging from as early as 10 a.m. to sleep onset as late as 2:45 p.m. Sleep diary record review revealed, on average, 7 hours of sleep overnight, with an additional hour during the day.

The clinical interview and sleep diary revealed that Darcy did not fall asleep independently, she exhibited excessive sleep onset delay, required assistance to resume sleep during night waking and that she was achieving insufficient total sleep time. It was my clinical impression that Darcy presented with: Insomnia; Behavioral Insomnia of Childhood, Sleep Onset Association Type. The following protocol was established with Darcy's parents after discussing the options for teaching Darcy to fall asleep independently. Darcy's parents expressed concern for disrupting the sleep of her older siblings as well as their puppy thereby opting out of the cry-it-out and other extinction-based protocols.

Sleep Protocol for Darcy

We are working to teach Darcy to sleep between 8 p.m. and 6 a.m. at night with a nap between noon and 3 p.m. We will do this by making sure she is ready to fall asleep when she is placed in bed, ensuring her room is quiet and dark at bedtime, and moving her bedtime gradually to work with her body. To make sure she is ready to fall asleep, we will control when she goes to bed and when she wakes up. Below is the protocol we discussed.

1. Bedtime at 9 p.m.
    a. Do bedtime routine just before bedtime.
    b. Rock Darcy for the duration of one song then place her in her crib and shut off music.
    c. Stand or sit next to Darcy until she falls asleep.
    d. Occasionally praise/touch Darcy for lying quietly.
    e. If she stands/cries, lay her down and tell her it is time to sleep.
2. Include blanket in rocking, cuddling, consoling and at bedtime and naps at home.
3. When Darcy wakes in the night, go to her and follow routine employed at bedtime.
    a. Dilute milk with water an ounce at a time every two nights until water only.
        i) 7 oz milk/1 oz water
        ii) 6 oz milk/2 oz water
        iii) 5 oz milk/3 oz water

4. Keep morning wake consistent at 6 a.m.
5. Limit naps to 1.5 hours.
   a. Do not let Darcy nap past 3 p.m.
   b. Talk with child care provider.
6. Once Darcy falls asleep within 20 minutes of bedtime with a parent present (not holding her) for three consecutive nights implement the excuse-me drill beginning the fourth night (see attached description).
   a. Keep bedtime at 9 p.m.
7. After Darcy falls asleep alone in her room within 20 minutes of bedtime for 3 nights in a row, move bedtime 15 minutes earlier.
8. Repeat step 7 and hold bedtime at 8 p.m.
9. Hang up black out curtains to eliminate light exposure at nap, bedtime and early morning.
10. Complete sleep diary.
11. E-mail an update in 3 days.

Darcy's father returned to the follow-up appointment 1 week later and reported minimal implementation of the sleep protocol and minimal improvement in Darcy's sleep. He described following the recommendations for diluting her milk and that during the week Darcy discontinued requests for milk. Darcy's father reported the napping schedule had become more consistent. He added that he occasionally put Darcy in bed "nearly or barely" asleep rather than rocking her until she was sound asleep. He noted this occurred two of the last six nights. He reported that they continued to rock Darcy during night wakings and sleeping through the night in the chair with her following her second night waking. The sleep diary revealed Darcy was sleeping till 6 a.m. more often compared to baseline. Darcy's father further disclosed that his wife and children were out of town until the next day and expressed interest in implementing the cry-it-out procedure. We discussed the pros and cons of this procedure and how to manage implementation on subsequent nights when his wife and children were back home. Darcy's father agreed to the protocol change and to be in contact daily. The protocol remained the same with the exception of placing Darcy in bed and allowing her to cry till asleep and to cry herself back to sleep during night wakings. Subsequent telephone contact with Darcy's father revealed Darcy cried for approximately 40 minutes the first night, 15 minutes the second

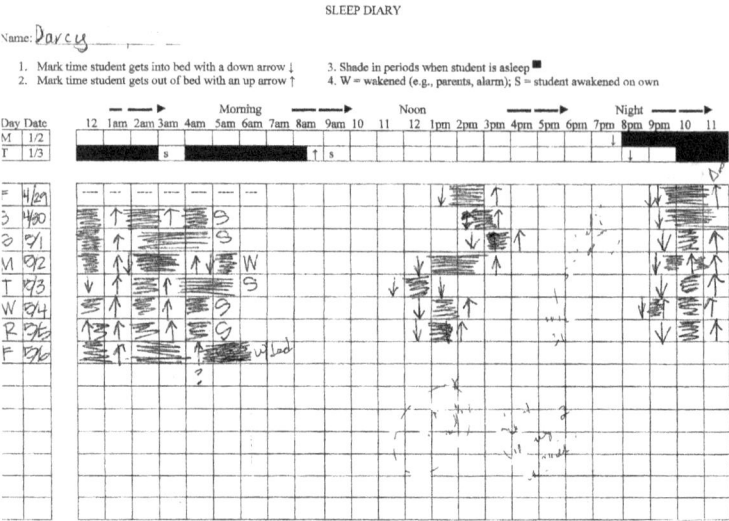

Figure 5.3 Baseline sleep diary: Darcy

night, and less than 10 minutes the third night. He also reported, Darcy slept through the night beginning the first night and was sleeping till 6 a.m. He and his wife were very pleased with Darcy's progress. A portion of the baseline and the follow-up sleep diaries are presented in Figures 5.3 and 5.4.

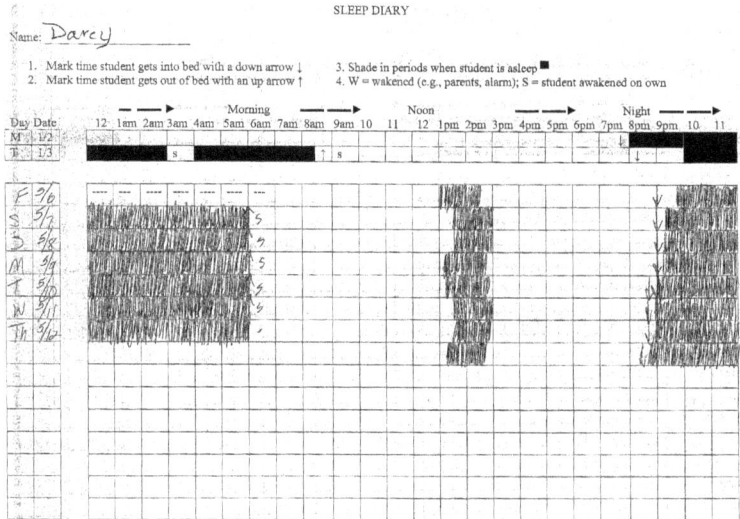

Figure 5.4 Follow-up sleep diary: Darcy

Insomnia

Isaiah

Isaiah was a 13-year-old African American male. He lived with his parents and one younger brother. Isaiah and his mother presented to clinic for concerns related to delayed sleep onset and excessive daytime sleepiness. Isaiah was born with spina bifida that resulted in complications related to his gastrointestinal (GI) system. He participated in outpatient behavioral health services as toddler to assist with potty training. Isaiah's medical history was remarkable for upper and lower GI scopes and a colonoscopy due to chronic GI problems associated with spina bifida. Isaiah had been hospitalized multiple times for constipation and clean-out procedures, most recently 3 years ago. He was prescribed fiber and MiraLAX as well as probiotics to help manage and prevent constipation. He also reported frequent broken bones throughout childhood however he had not had any in the 8 months preceding his intake. Isaiah had seasonal allergies and took Zyrtec and Singulair daily. He was also prescribed a nasal spray that he was reluctant to take due to the uncomfortable sensation of putting something in his nose. Isaiah had his esophagus scraped and nose surgery to reduce the size of his turbinates. Isaiah's mother reported Isaiah was evaluated and diagnosed with sleep apnea and that consideration for a tonsillectomy, adenoidectomy, and Continuous positive airway pressure (CPAP) had been discussed but not yet pursued. She explained they were referred for outpatient behavioral sleep treatment as the next step for Isaiah. Isaiah was actively involved in three soccer teams and a basketball team.

The clinical interview revealed Isaiah went to bed at approximately 9:30 p.m. and was not asleep before 10 or 10:30 p.m. nightly with 10:30 p.m. more common. He reported waking nightly between 2 and 3 a.m. to use the bathroom, with morning wake at 6:40 a.m. His mother described difficulty waking him in the morning. Discussion of Isaiah's bedtime routine revealed poor hygiene, including sleeping in his after-school clothes, engaging in electronic activities in his bedroom, and having the TV or music on when he attempted to go to sleep. He also reported napping and being tired throughout the day. Isaiah and his mother revealed that Isaiah had only been sleeping in his bed for approximately

1 week, previously sleeping on the couch for approximately a month. Isaiah and his mother reported that sleeping on the couch began when he was sleeping sitting up, as he was experiencing difficulty breathing while lying down. Isaiah reported no current difficulties breathing lying down to go to sleep and attributed his previous difficulties to allergies. No other concerns related to daytime functioning were reported.

A sleep diary was completed for the 5 weeks prior to the intake appointment. Review of the diary revealed a variable bedtime schedule ranging from 9 p.m. to as late as 1:30 a.m., with a most common bedtime of 9:30 p.m. Sleep onset latency was variable ranging from, at the shortest, 30 minutes to, at the longest, 3 hours, with the most common onset latency of 1 hour and an average onset latency of 1.75 hours. The sleep diary also revealed a fairly consistent morning wake at 6:30 to 6:40 a.m., with occasional sleeping in until 8 a.m. and one morning sleeping as late as 9 a.m. The sleep diary revealed that Isaiah experienced night wakings on six nights, with frequent wakings on four of those nights. Although he recalled trouble sleeping some nights, Isaiah could not recall the details of specific wakings. His mother described them as hearing him up and down a lot. Following two of those nights, he stayed home from school due to excessive fatigue from limited sleep. The sleep diary also revealed frequent napping during the first four of the 5 weeks with naps on 15 days, ranging in duration from 30 minutes to 4.5 hours, with the most common duration 2 hours. Average overnight sleep time was 10:30 p.m. to 6:30 a.m. Isaiah's average total sleep time overnight was approximately 7.5 hours with wakings accounted for. His average daily total sleep time was 8.5 hours due to the additional, on average, hour of sleep gained from naps.

The clinical interview and sleep diary review revealed Isaiah experienced excessive sleep onset latency and frequent night wakings. Contributing to his insomnia were poor sleep hygiene and historical difficulties related to breathing. Consequences of his insomnia were sleep deprivation, sleepiness during the day, and napping at inappropriate times. As Isaiah's difficulties were discussed, psychoeducation was provided and the sleep protocol was developed. We discussed the importance of monitoring Isaiah's response to treatment in terms of decreased fatigue with increased sleep time to ensure that the quality of his sleep was adequate. The sleep protocol developed is provided below.

Sleep Protocol for Isaiah

We are working to teach Isaiah to sleep between 9 p.m. and 6:30 a.m. at night. We will do this by making sure he is ready to fall asleep when he goes to bed, ensuring his room is quiet and dark at bedtime, and moving his bedtime gradually to work with his body. To make sure he is ready to fall asleep we will control when he goes to bed and when he wakes up. We are also working to teach his brain and his body when it is time to sleep. We will do this by limiting his daytime activities in his bedroom. Following is the protocol we discussed.

1. Bedtime at 10:30 p.m.
   a. Do bedtime routine just before bedtime.
   b. Put pajamas on just before bed.
   c. Keep room quiet and dark.
2. Move electronics (Play Station, computer, TV) out of bedroom.
   a. Watch TV, listen to music, text, play games, watch videos, and so on outside of bedroom.
   b. Until dad can help move electronics spend limited amount of time in bedroom unless in bed to sleep.
3. Nothing but sleep in bed.
   a. Sleep only in bed, not on couch, in car, and so on.
4. Keep morning wake consistent at 6:30 a.m.
5. Move bedtime 15 minutes earlier after falling asleep three nights in a row within 20 minutes.
6. Repeat step 5 and hold bedtime at 9 p.m.
   a. Follow schedule closely until 9 or 9:30 p.m. to 6:30 a.m. schedule is in place for 2 weeks including weekends.
7. No napping.
8. Complete sleep diary.
9. E-mail an update in 3 days.

Isaiah and his mother returned to clinic 1 week later with a sleep diary. Discussion revealed good adherence to the sleep protocol, with less difficulty than anticipated by Isaiah and his mother. Isaiah was commended for his follow-through. The sleep diary revealed that the current bedtime was 10:15 p.m., with sleep onset occurring within 15 minutes. In the past week, he had one night with disrupted sleep that he attributed to severe migraines, resulting in at least 3 hours of wake time during the night and not attending school the next day. The sleep diary also revealed a more variable morning wake schedule due to the holiday. We discussed the importance of maintaining the schedule. Isaiah also napped during 2- to 3-hour car rides at the beginning of the week. He had not napped since. We reviewed the components of the sleep diary. Isaiah completed an Epworth Sleepiness Scale and Epworth Fatigue Scale. I discussed with Isaiah and his mother barriers to utilizing nasal spray treatment for his allergies and potential contributions to his more severe headaches this past week. No changes were made to the protocol.

Isaiah and his mother returned 2 weeks later. The sleep diary they presented revealed good adherence to the sleep protocol, with ready sleep onset. Current bedtime was 9:15 p.m. Morning wake was consistent at 6:30 a.m., with a later wake time one morning. Isaiah had taken four naps. Two of the naps were a little bit longer due to long car rides, and the other two naps were 30 minutes and 15 minutes in duration. One night he had an extended night waking related to a dangerous situation at his brother's college campus and frequent phone call alerts. Isaiah completed an Epworth Sleepiness Scale and Epworth Fatigue Scale. It demonstrated improvement in his daytime sleepiness Total score improved from 6 to 4 with zero items endorsed at a 2 or higher on the follow-up scale. The total score for daytime fatigue improved from a 22 to 14. I reviewed with Isaiah what he learned through the process and what he might do in the future should his sleep become disrupted. The follow-up plan was to obtain another set of an Epworth Sleepiness and Epworth Fatigue Scales in 10 days after Isaiah achieved a 9 p.m. to 6:30 a.m. sleep schedule for a week. Isaiah and his mother left the appointment with the scales and agreed to complete and return them as no further appointments were scheduled due to his progress and adherence. The scales were never received and no further complaints were reported. Samples of Isaiah's baseline and the final follow-up sleep diaries are presented in Figures 5.5 and 5.6.

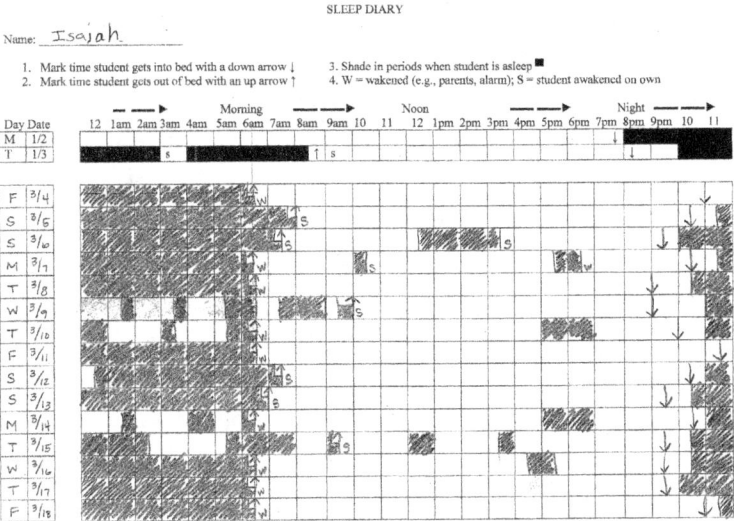

Figure 5.5 Baseline sleep diary: Isaiah

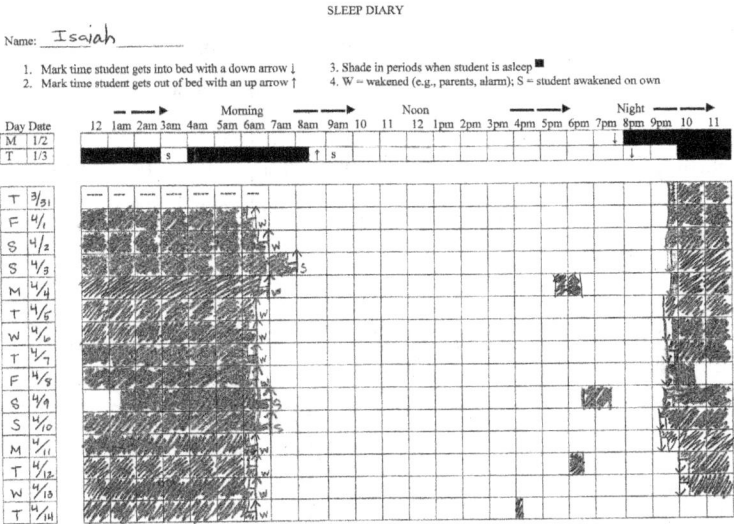

Figure 5.6 Follow-up sleep diary: Isaiah

Co-Occurring Sleep Disturbance and Anxiety

Helena was a 12-year-old Caucasian female. She lived with her parents and younger brother (age 10). Helena and her family relocated from out of state 2 years prior to presenting to clinic. Helena's medical history was remarkable for difficulties with stomachaches and headaches with no detectable medical cause other than lactose intolerance. Helena and her mother sought services for concerns related to anxiety and its negative impact on her sleep.

Helena's psychiatric history was remarkable for outpatient psychological services when she was in the second grade for concerns related to anxiety resulting in diagnoses of Attention Deficit Hyperactivity Disorder (ADHD) and anxiety. Helena began treatment with methylphenidate extended release 10 mg qid and sertraline 25 mg qid with continued treatment since that time. Helena's mother reported a recent increased dose for sertraline (50 mg) and drug holidays from methylphenidate during the summers and 1-week recently. The recent drug holiday from methylphenidate was to assess its benefit. Helena reported increased difficulty staying organized, remembering information, and staying focused. In addition, Helena participated in outpatient services upon relocating 2 years ago per her prescriber's recommendation. Helena attended three or four sessions for concerns related to the transition as well as sleep concerns with minimal therapeutic benefit gain from the services. Helena participated in outpatient services a year later with another provider for concerns specifically related to sleep. Helena did not exhibit consistent independent sleep onset skills and was having difficulty falling asleep and remaining asleep throughout the night. The services were reportedly discontinued after several weeks due to the focus on sleep rather than anxiety and limited progress related to the sleep concerns

The clinical interview revealed primary concern with anxiety and its impact on Helena's ability to develop independent sleep onset skills and sustain sleep throughout the night. Helena reported her sleep onset latency was approximately 30 to 45 minutes, that she rarely fell asleep alone in her own room and required the presence of one of her parents. Helena reported she also woke nightly at approximately 1 a.m. and struggled to go back to sleep most nights for 60 to 90 minutes. Helena's mother reported Helena solicited her or her father to come to Helena's bedroom to help her go back to sleep. Helena's mother described resisting going to Helena's bedroom until she had been awake for 60 to 90 minutes. Once a parent was present Helena fell asleep within 5 minutes.

Helena's mother described that the master bedroom was on the main floor and Helena's bedroom was on the second floor of their home. Helena described feeling very fearful and "freaking out" when she had to go downstairs to her parents' bedroom when she awoke in the night. An extra room on the second floor was converted into a bedroom to enable Helena to seek her parents' assistance across the hall. Helena reported being less fearful in the night; however, she was still not able to fall back asleep unless a parent came into her room. Sharing a bedroom with her brother also failed to resolve the problem as Helena liked the light on and her brother preferred to sleep in the dark. In addition, when he woke in the night to use the bathroom, Helena would wake and was unable to resume sleep.

Helena's morning wake time was 6:30 to 6:45 a.m. three out of five school mornings, 5:45 a.m. the other two mornings and 7 or 8 a.m. on weekends. Helena was achieving 6.5 to 7 hours of sleep on a good school night, with less than 6 hours of sleep two nights a week and approximately 7 to 7.5 hours of sleep on weekends. This was well below recommended norms for a child Helena's age.

The clinical interview also revealed Helena exhibited symptoms of panic associated with fears related to something bad happening to her, such as getting cancer, or something terrible happening to her parents or to her brother. Panic symptoms included sweating, trembling, swallowing air resulting in a stomachache, increased breathing rate, and a rapid pounding heartbeat. The panic symptoms typically occurred when Helena was more distressed or tired, and that was typically in the evening and at bedtime. Thoughts related to "what if something terrible happens" were common when Helena was trying to go to sleep (three or four times per week) and had been present for 4 months. Helena was able to manage rapid breathing during the school day without increased symptoms. Additional anxiety or fears related to other people getting hurt beyond her parents, brother, and friends resulted in Helena avoiding watching TV due to advertisements for scary movies or news clips that revealed violence and triggered worry that something similar would happen to her family or herself.

The clinical interview revealed Helena experienced significant symptoms of anxiety in addition to the absence of independent sleep onset skills, insufficient total sleep time, and poor sleep hygiene. The initial diagnoses included: Unspecified Anxiety Disorder; Insomnia; Behavioral Insomnia of Childhood, Sleep Onset Association Type; and Panic Disorder. The anxiety diagnosis was later revised to obsessive compulsive disorder.

Helena participated in 10 outpatient appointments that were scheduled weekly to monthly over the course of treatment. Treatment initially focused on anxiety with exposure and response prevention the primary treatment modality. Helena's primary treatment goal was related to establishing independent sleep onset skills. Although Helena's sleep behavior and fears related to sleep were discussed at every appointment, initial treatment recommendations focused on daytime obsessions and compulsions. Helena was cooperative during sessions and followed through with treatment recommendations. It was evident through her report and nonverbal response that discussions of going to bed and falling asleep independently generated her most intense fear response.

Four months into treatment at Helena's sixth session, Helena's sleep behavior was discussed in detail with the intent of developing a specific sleep protocol. Helena was reluctant to take this step during previous sessions. Previous sessions resulted in generating Helena's rationales for achieving independent sleep onset with a recommendation for daily exposure via reading the rationales in an effort to increase Helena's motivation to address sleep directly. Although Helena did not implement this exposure strategy, she returned with a completed sleep diary. The sleep diary revealed an approximately 60-minute sleep onset latency most nights with at least one night waking on a nightly basis, 60 minutes in duration. Helena had continued to call out for her parents and when they failed to respond to her requests Helena moved to her brother's room.

In establishing a specific sleep protocol sleep hygiene issues, nothing but sleep in bed and practicing relaxation procedures in bed during the day and at bedtime were addressed. Helena was less reactive when the topic of sleep intervention was introduced at the sixth session compared to previous sessions. As the focus shifted to the details of the sleep protocol Helena appeared more distraught and was coached to remind herself of the benefits of achieving independent sleep onset skills and the temporary nature of the cost (i.e., anxiety). The protocol provided below was established with Helena and her mother.

Sleep Protocol for Helena

We are working to teach Helena to sleep between 10:30 p.m. and 8 a.m. We will do this by making sure she is ready to fall asleep when she goes to bed, ensuring her room is quiet and dark at bedtime and teaching her body to relax when she is in bed. To make sure she is ready to fall asleep, we will control when she goes to bed and when she wakes up. Below is the protocol we discussed.

1. Helena is to practice deep breathing (inhale through nose for count of 4, hold for count of 4, exhale through mouth for count of 4, hold for count of 4, repeat) in her bed 2 to 3 times daily and at bedtime.
2. Bedtime at 11 p.m.
   a. Do bedtime routine just before bedtime.
   b. Put pajamas on just before bed.
   c. Review day before bedtime with a parent.
3. Nothing but sleep (and relaxation) in bed.
4. Keep room quiet (sound machine is okay) and dark.
5. Mother to remain in Helena's bedroom on a chair or the floor until Helena falls asleep.
   a. Do not lay in bed with Helena.
6. When Helena wakes in the night, mother is to return to Helena's bedroom and sit on a chair until Helena falls asleep.
   a. Helena is to get her mother immediately when she wakes in the night.
7. Keep morning wake consistent at 8 a.m.
8. Complete sleep diary.
9. E-mail update in 3 days.

At the seventh session, 1 week later, Helena and her mother reported following through with the sleep protocol specifically: mother remaining in the room next to the bed until Helena fell asleep, an 11 p.m. bedtime, Helena waking her parents upon night wakings, and completing a sleep diary. The sleep diary revealed immediate sleep onset every night. Helena's mother reported that on three occasions, Helena attempted to convince her to lie in bed with Helena and she resisted two nights. Helena's mother reported that the previous evening, Helena came in twice and was awake for a more extended period of time the second time. Helena reported delaying retrieving her mother the second time that she awoke. She was encouraged to immediately get her mother as stated in the protocol. I employed cognitive strategies and motivational interviewing techniques to facilitate motivation to follow-through with the protocol to achieve Helena's identified goals of learning to fall asleep independently. We established that with the family leaving town on Wednesday, they should continue current procedures on Sunday and Monday upon return and introduce the "excuse-me" drill protocol on Tuesday. We revised the sleep protocol and reviewed each step in detail. An incentive was established to motivate Helena to resist asking her mother to lie in bed with her the next week for three nights. The steps listed below were added to the sleep protocol.

1. Starting Tuesday (after the holiday) implement the excuse-me drill.
   a. Bedtime is still 11 p.m.
2. Match night-waking response to bedtime process.
3. Incentive for resisting asking mother to get in bed for three nights = Hawaiian Ice.

The eighth session occurred 2 weeks later. The sleep diary and verbal report indicated following the 11 p.m. bedtime most nights and the protocol provided. Helena's mother reported implementing the excuse-me drill as of Tuesday evening as planned with Helena doing a sleepover Wednesday evening. Helena reported resisting asking her mother to lay with her until Thursday evening when she felt nauseous due to eating dairy given her lactose intolerance. We reset her goal for an incentive for not asking her mother to lay with her. Discussed continued implementation of the excuse-me drill and holding the sleep schedule at 11 p.m. to 8 a.m. Helena also reported that she had not read the exposure cards regarding independent sleep; provided psychoeducation regarding her avoidance of this assignment; and employed cognitive strategies to facilitate follow-through.

The ninth session occurred 1 month later. Helena was pleased to report that she was much more independent in her sleep routine. Her mother described that Helena had been getting ready for bed and going to bed independently. Her mother reported delaying entering Helena's room for approximately 15 minutes after Helena went to bed, sitting in Helena's room for 1 to 2 minutes and leaving. She reported returning approximately 15 minutes later and most often found Helena asleep. Helena reported that she woke this morning and was tempted to go get her mother, but simply went to the bathroom, went back to bed, and went back to sleep. Her progress was enthusiastically praised. Helena expressed a sense of accomplishment with regard to her progress. We reviewed functioning across domains and Helena demonstrated maintenance of progress, with the exception of Internet searching for health concerns. Strategies for managing this compulsive behavior were reviewed.

The tenth session occurred a few months later. Helena and her mother reported Helena maintained progress in areas associated with anxiety initially demonstrated, specifically decreased mirror-checking, decreased weighing of herself, decreased concern about what she wears to school, and decreased worry for her brother's reputation and eating habits. They noted continued struggles with her own health and checking the Internet repeatedly to explain medical symptoms that she anticipated experiencing. We discussed one event that resulted in a trip to the emergency room. We established limits for Internet-checking to one time per week and only following gathering parental impressions of her symptoms. Follow-up on sleep revealed that Helena was going to bed independently on a nightly basis, occasionally waking in the night and moving to her brother's room, as opposed to staying in her own room. Reviewed the importance of remaining in her own room in order to establish the ability to do so. Helena expressed understanding and willingness to work toward that goal.

A telephone contact with Helena's mother a few months later revealed continued struggles with occasional night wakings that resulted in Helena moving to her brother's bedroom. Helena's mother expressed satisfaction with the amount of progress Helena had made. We agreed she would follow up in a couple of months if additional appointments were needed. I encouraged her to let Helena know that I was eager to hear that she was sleeping in her own bed all night. No further appointments were scheduled. Portions of the baseline and follow-up sleep diaries are presented in Figures 5.7 and 5.8.

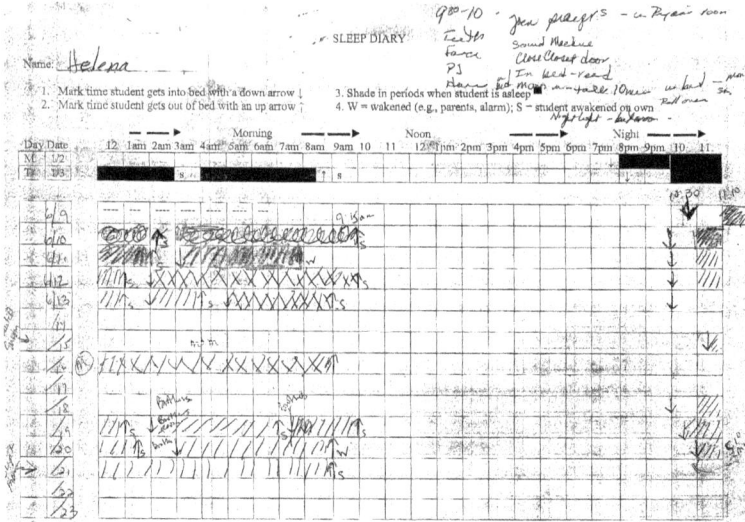

Figure 5.7 Baseline sleep diary: Helena

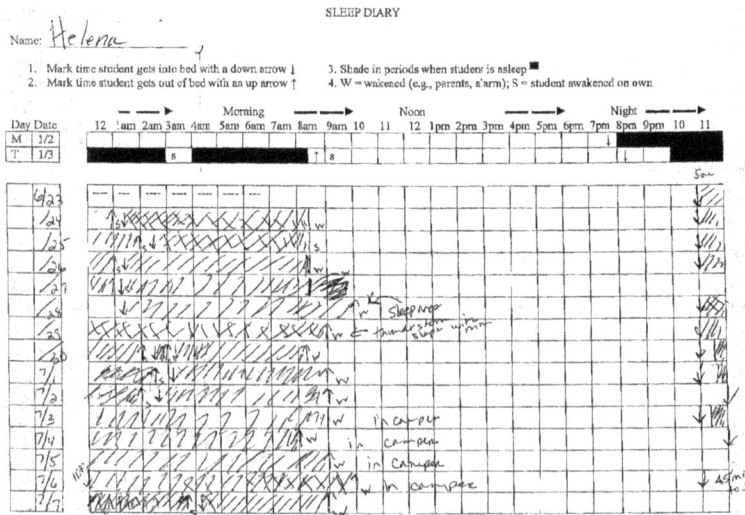

Figure 5.8 Follow-up sleep diary: Helena

References

American Academy of Sleep Medicine (AASM). 2005. *The International Classification of Sleep Disorders, Diagnostic and Coding Manual* second edition, Westchester, IL: American Academy of Sleep Medicine.

American Academy of Sleep Medicine (AASM). 2014. *The International Classification of Sleep Disorders, Diagnostic and Coding Manual* third edition, Westchester, IL: American Academy of Sleep Medicine.

American Psychiatric Association. 2013. *Diagnostic and Statistical Manual of Mental Disorders, Fifth Edition (DSM-5)*. Washington, DC: American Psychiatric Publishing.

Beebe, Dean W. 2011. "Cognitive, Behavioral, and Functional Consequences of Inadequate Sleep in Children and Adolescents." *Pediatric Clinics of North America 58: 649–665.*

Beebe, Dean W., and David Gozal. 2002. "Obstructive Sleep Apnea and the Prefrontal Cortex: Towards a Comprehensive Model Linking Nocturnal Upper Airway Obstruction to Daytime Cognitive and Behavioral Deficits." *Journal of Sleep Research* 11: 1–16.

Burke, Raymond. V., Brett Kuhn, and Janie L. Peterson. 2004. "A "Storybook" Ending to Children's Bedtime Problems: The Use of a Rewarding Social Story to Reduce Bedtime Resistance and Frequent Night Waking." *Journal of Pediatric Psychology* 29: 389–396.

Dahl, Ronald E. 1996. "The Impact of Inadequate Sleep on Children's Daytime Cognitive Function." *Seminars in Pediatric Neurology* 3:44–50.

Eliasson, Arne, Joseph King, and Ben Gould. 2002. "Association of Sleep and Academic Performance." *Sleep and Breathing* 6:45–48.

Ferber, Richard. 2006. *Solve Your Child's Sleep Problems: New Revised and Expanded Edition.* New York, NY: Simon and Schuster.

Freeman, Kurt A. 2006. "Treating Bedtime Resistance with Bedtime Pass: A Systematic Replication and Component Analysis with 3-Year Olds." *Journal of Applied Behavior Analysis* 3:423–428.

Friman, Patrick C., Kathryn E. Hoff, Connie Schnoes, Kurt A. Freeman, Douglas W. Woods, and Nathan Blum. 1999. "The Bedtime Pass: An Approach to Bedtime Crying and Leaving the Room." *Archives of Pediatric and Adolescent Medicine* 153:1027–1029.

Kennaway, David J. 2015. "Potential Safety Issues in the Use of the Hormone Melatonin in Paediatrics." *Journal of Paediatrics and Child Health* 51:584–589.

Kuhn, Brett R. 2011. "The Excuse-Me Drill: A Behavioral Protocol to Promote Independent Sleep Initiation Skills and Reduce Bedtime Problems in Young Children." In *Behavioral Treatments for Sleep Disorders: A Comprehensive Primer of Behavioral Sleep Medicine Interventions,* edited by Michael Perlis, Mark Aloia, and Brett Kuhn 299–310. Boston, MA: Elsevier.

Kuhn, Brett R., and Amy J. Elliott. 2003. "Treatment Efficacy in Behavioral Pediatric Sleep Medicine. *Journal of Psychosomatic Research* 54:587–597

Lewandowski, Amy S. Marisol Toliver-Sokol, and Tonya M. Palermo. 2011. "Evidence-Based Review of Subjective Pediatric Sleep Measures." *Journal of Pediatric Psychology* 36:1–14.

Meltzer, Lisa J., and Jodi A. Mindell. 2006. "Sleep, Sleep Disorders in Children and Adolescents." *Pediatric Clinics of North America* 29:1059–1076.

Melendres, M. C., J. M. Lutz, E. D. Rubin, and C. L. Marcus. 2004. "Daytime Sleepiness and Hyperactivity in Children with Suspected Sleep Disordered Breathing." *Pediatrics* 114: 768–775.

Mindell, Jodi A. 1999. "Empirically Supported Treatments in Pediatric Psychology: Bedtime Refusal and Night Wakings in Young Children." *Journal of Pediatric Psychology* 24:465–481.

Mindell, Jodi A., Brett Kuhn, Daniel S. Lewin, Lisa J. Meltzer, and Avi Sadeh. 2006. "Behavioral Treatment of Bedtime Problems and Night Wakings in Infants and Young Children." *Sleep* 29:1263–1276.

Mindell, Jodi A., and Judith A. Owens. 2003. *A Clinical Guide to Pediatric Sleep: Diagnosis and Management of Sleep Problems.* Philadelphia, PA: Lippincott, Williams and Wilkins.

Moore Brie A., Patrick C. Friman, Alan E. Fruzzetti, and Ken MacAleese K. 2007. "Evaluating the Bedtime Pass Program for Child Resistance to Bedtime: A Randomized, Controlled Trial." *Journal of Pediatric Psychology* 32:283–287.

National Center for Health Statistics. 2010. "International Statistical Classification of Diseases and Related Health Problems, 10th Revision, Clinical Modification (ICD-10-CM)." Centers for Disease Control and Prevention (CDC).

National Sleep Foundation. 2006. *Sleep in America Poll.* Washington, DC: American Academy of Sleep Medicine.

Owens, Judith A., Anthony Spirito, and Melissa McGuinn. 2000. "The Children's Sleep Habits Questionnaire (CSHQ): Psychometric Properties of a Survey Instrument for School-Aged Children." *Sleep* 23:1–9.

Owens, Judith A, Carol L. Rosen, and Jodi A. Mindell. 2003. "Medication Use in the Treatment of Pediatric Insomnia: Results of a Survey of Community-Based Pediatricians." *Pediatrics* 111:e628–635.

Owens Judith, A., and Victoria Dalzell. 2005. "Use of the 'BEARS' Sleep Screening Tool in a Pediatric Residents' Continuity Clinic: A Pilot Study." *Sleep Medicine* 6:63–69.

Peterson, Janie, and Macy Peterson. 2003. *The Sleep Fairy*. Omaha, NE: Behave'n Kids Press, Inc.

Randazzo Angela C., Mark J. Muehlbach, Paula K. Schweitzer, and James K. Walsh. 1998. "Cognitive Function Following Acute Sleep Restriction in Children Ages 10–14." *Sleep* 21:861–868.

Rosen, Carol L., Judith A. Owens, and Jodi A. Mindell. 2005. "Use of Pharmacotherapy for Insomnia in Children and Adolescents: A National Survey of Child Psychiatrists." *Sleep* 28:A79.

Schnoes, Connie J. 2017. *The Bedtime Pass*. Omaha, NE: Moose Tracks Publishing.

Schnoes, Connie J. 2011. "The Bedtime Pass." In *Behavioral Treatments for Sleep Disorders: A Comprehensive Primer of Behavioral Sleep Medicine Interventions*, edited by Michael Perlis, Mark Aloia, and Brett Kuhn 293–298. Boston, MA: Elsevier.

Schnoes, Connie J., Brett R. Kuhn, Eliza F. Workman, and Cynthia R. Ellis. 2006. "Pediatric Prescribing Practices for Clonidine and Other Pharmacologic Agents for Children with Sleep Disturbance." *Clinical Pediatrics* 45:229–238.

Smaldone, Arlene, Judy C. Honig, and Mary W. Byrne. 2007. "Sleepless in America: Inadequate Sleep and Relationships to Health and Well-being of Our Nation's Children." *Pediatrics* 119:s29–s37. Accessed June 6, 2016. DOI: 10.1542/peds.2006-2089F.

Spruyt, Karen, and David Gozal. 2011. "Pediatric Sleep Questionnaires as Diagnostic or Epidemiological Tools: A Review of Currently Available Instruments." *Sleep Medicine Review* 5:19–32.

Sulit, Loreto G., Amy Storfer-Isser, Carol L. Rosen, H. Lester Kirchner, and Susan Redline. 2005. "Associations of Obesity, Sleep-disordered Breathing, and Wheezing in Children." *American Journal of Respiratory and Critical Care Medicine* 171:659–664.

Wolfson, Amy R., and Mary A. Carskadon. 1998. "Sleep Schedules and Daytime Functioning in Adolescents." *Child Development* 69:875–887.

About the Author

Dr. Connie J. Schnoes is a licensed psychologist who provides direct clinical services to children and families at the Boys Town Center for Behavioral Health. Dr. Schnoes conducted the original study demonstrating efficacy of the bedtime pass. She has been involved in conducting sleep research and delivering clinical services for sleep disorders for 20 years. She has published research articles and book chapters, presented at national conferences, conducted press interviews and recorded informative videos on the topic of sleep. She is a member of the American Academy of Sleep Medicine. She provides training and supervision of doctoral psychology interns and post-doctoral fellows on the topic of sleep and sleep disturbance. She is also engaged in the replication of outpatient behavioral health services nationally for Boys Town.

Index

OTHER TITLES IN OUR CHILD CLINICAL PSYCHOLOGY "NUTS AND BOLTS" COLLECTION

Samuel T. Gontkovsky, *Editor*

- *Learning Disabilities* by Charles J. Golden and Lisa K. Lashley
- *Intellectual Disabilities* by Charles J. Golden and Lisa K. Lashley
- *A Guide for Statistics in the Behavioral Sciences* by Jeff Foster

FORTHCOMING TITLES IN THIS COLLECTION

- *Childhood and Adolescent Obesity* by Lauren A Stutts
- *Depression in Childhood and Adolescence: A Guide for Practitioners* by Rebecca A. Schwartz-Mette, Cynthia A. Erdley, Douglas W. Nangle, and Hannah Lawrence
- *Elimination Disorders: Evidence Based Treatment for Enuresis and Encopresis* by Thomas Reimers

Momentum Press offers over 30 collections including Aerospace, Biomedical, Civil, Environmental, Nanomaterials, Geotechnical, and many others. We are a leading book publisher in the field of engineering, mathematics, health, and applied sciences.

Momentum Press is actively seeking collection editors as well as authors. For more information about becoming an MP author or collection editor, please visit http://www.momentumpress.net/contact

Announcing Digital Content Crafted by Librarians

Concise e-books business students need for classroom and research

Momentum Press offers digital content as authoritative treatments of advanced engineering topics by leaders in their field. Hosted on ebrary, MP provides practitioners, researchers, faculty, and students in engineering, science, and industry with innovative electronic content in sensors and controls engineering, advanced energy engineering, manufacturing, and materials science.

Momentum Press offers library-friendly terms:
- *perpetual access for a one-time fee*
- *no subscriptions or access fees required*
- *unlimited concurrent usage permitted*
- *downloadable PDFs provided*
- *free MARC records included*
- *free trials*

The **Momentum Press** digital library is very affordable, with no obligation to buy in future years.

For more information, please visit **www.momentumpress.net/library** or to set up a trial in the US, please contact **mpsales@globalepress.com**.

www.ingramcontent.com/pod-product-compliance
Lightning Source LLC
Chambersburg PA
CBHW050539270326
41926CB00015B/3294